interactive

Gibson ®

Bible

GIBSON FACTS

Jawbone

An imprint of Outline Press Ltd

2A Union Court, 20–22 Union Road,

London SW4 6JP, England

www.jawbonepress.com

ISBN: 978-1-906002-10-7

TEXT: Walter Carter, Dave Hunter
EDITOR: Pete Chrisp
DESIGN: Paul Cooper Design

Origination and print by Colorprint (Hong Kong)

1 2 3 4 5 12 11 10 09 08

contents

HOW TO USE THIS BOOK

The Gibson facts guidebook provides two groups of listings of virtually all the electric guitars to have carried the Gibson logo. Only a few low-run, limited edition models, and some models where few or no details were available, are not included.

The first group – pages 6 to 19 – is an A-to-Z listing of Gibson electric models from the 1930s to 2007. The second and main set of listings later in the book – pages 20 to 101 – organises the models by year of introduction and offers more detailed information.

To cross-reference a model in the A-to-Z listing with the later year-by-year listing, look up the first year of production in the A-to-Z and go to the relevant year in the chronological section.

In the A-to-Z listing, the seven most popular guitar types – Chet Atkins models, ES models, Explorer models, Firebird models, Flying V models, Les Paul models and SG models – have been issued in more variations and spin-offs than any other Gibson products and so have been separated and given their own headings, with each model listed alphabetically under that heading. All other Gibson models that do not fall within one of these seven groupings are then listed at the end of the A-to-Z section under 'Other Models' or 'Custom Models' and again listed alphabetically.

A note about Artist Signature models

Artist Signature models are listed at the end of each of the A-to-Z sections under the surname of the endorsing artist – eg Jimi Hendrix is listed under 'H'.

In the chronological section, Artist Signature guitars are listed alphabetically by their official model name – eg 'Jimi Hendrix Flying V' is listed under 'J', 'Bob Marley Les Paul Special' is listed under 'B' etc.

As a final cross-reference, in the index at the end of the book – pages 102–107 – all models are listed purely alphabetically, again with the seven most popular guitar types given their own headings. In the index, Artist Signature guitars are also listed alphabetically by their official model name – 'Jimi Hendrix Flying V' under 'J' etc etc.

models:
a–z

A–Z Listing

This A-Z listing is broken down into nine main model groupings as follows:

CHET ATKINS MODELS
ES MODELS
EXPLORER MODELS
FIREBIRD MODELS
FLYING V MODELS
LES PAUL MODELS
SG MODELS
OTHER MODELS
CUSTOM MODELS

Models are listed alphabetically within these groups except for Artist Signature models, which are listed separately at the end of each group, alphabetically by last name – (e.g. Jimi Hendrix = H).

Models with product or personality themes are listed under Custom models.

Production totals, where available, are from the personal records of Gibson employee Julius Bellson for the pre-World War II years (1937–41) and from Gibson shipping totals (1948–79).

CHET ATKINS MODELS

Chet Atkins 350XT: Prototype of Chet Atkins Country Gentleman.

Chet Atkins 3535: Original name for Chet Atkins Country Gentleman.

Chet Atkins CE (Standard) (1982–2005)

Chet Atkins CE Showcase Edition (July 1988 guitar of the month)

Chet Atkins CEC (1982–2005)

Chet Atkins CEC – True Cedar (2000–2005)

Chet Atkins CGP (1986–87)

Chet Atkins Country Gentleman (1986–2005)

Chet Atkins (JS) Double (1989–91)

Chet Atkins Phasar (1987)

Chet Atkins SST (1987–2005)

Chet Atkins SST 12-string (1990–94)

Chet Atkins SST 12-string Brett Michaels Edition (1992–93)

Chet Atkins SST Celebrity Series (1991–93)

Chet Atkins SST – True Cedar (2000–2005)

Chet Atkins SST w/flame-top (1993–95)

Chet Atkins Studio CE (1993–2000, 2004–05)

Chet Atkins Studio CEC (1993–2000, 2004–05)

Chet Atkins Studio Classic (1991–93)

Chet Atkins Super 4000 (1995, 1997)

Chet Atkins Tennessean (1990–2005)

ES MODELS

ES-5 (1949–55)
ES-5 Reissue (1996–2006)
ES-5 Switchmaster (1955–62)

Switchmaster Reissue (1996–2006)
Switchmaster Reissue Alnico (1996–2006)

ES-100 (1938–41)/ **ES-125** pre-WWII (1941–43)
EST-100 / ETG-100 (1940–41): 4-string tenor. Production: 19.

ES-120T (1962–70)

ES-125 pre-WWII. See ES-100.
ES-125 post-WWII (1946–70)
ES-125C (1966–70)
ES-125CD (1966–70)
ES-125T (1956–68)
ES-125T (¾-scale) (1957–68)
ES-125TC (1961–69)
ES-125TCD (1960)
ES-125TD (1957–63)
ES-125TDC (1961–70)

ES-130 full-depth (1954–56), **ES-135** (1956–57)

ES-135 2nd version (1991–2003)
ES-135 Gothic (1998–99)
Swingmaster ES-135 (1999)

ES-137 Classic (2002–current)
ES-137 Custom (2002–current)
ES-137P (Premier) (2002–04)

ES-140 (¾-scale) (1950–56)
ES-140T (¾-scale T) (1957–67)

ES-150 pre-WWII (1936–42)
EST-150 (1937–39) / ETG-150
    (1940–42)
ESP-150 (1939)
ES-150 post-WWII (1947–56)
ETG-150 (1947–71)
ES-150DC (1969–74)

ES-175 single pickup (1949–72)
ES-175 double pickup (1951–53,
    1971–91, 2006–current) / ES-175D
    (1953–70) / ES-175 Reissue
    (1991–2005)
ES-175 Aged Reissue (2002–04)
ES-175CC (1978–79)
ES-175D CMT (1989–90)
ES-175T (1976–79)
Swingmaster ES-175 (1999)

ES-225T (1956–58)
ES-225TD (1956–59): 2 pickups.
    Production: 2,754.

ES-240 (1977–1978)

ES-250 (1939–40)

ES-295 (1952–58, 1990–2000)

ES-300 pre-WWII (1940–42)
ES-300 post-WWII (1945–52)

ES-320TD (1971–74)

ES-325TD (1972–79)

ES-330T (1959–63)

ES-330TD (1959–71) (1998–99)

ES-333 (2003–05)

ES-335TD (1958–81) / ES-335 DOT
    (1981–90) / ES-335 Reissue
    (1991–98) / ES-335 Dot
    (1999–current)
1959 ES-335 DOT Reissue
    (2002–current)
1963 ES-335 Block Reissue
    (2002–current)
Custom Shop ES-335 (1995–2001)
ES-335-12 (1965–70)
ES-335 Block (1998–2000)
ES-335 Centennial (Aug. 1994 guitar
    of the month)
ES-335 CRR (1979)
ES-335 CRRS (1979)
ES-335 Custom: See Custom Shop
    ES-335.
ES-335 DOT (1981–90)
ES-335 DOT CMT (1983–85)
ES-335 Gothic (1998)
ES-335 Plain '60s Block (2005)
ES-335 Pro (1979–81)
ES-335 Reissue (1990–current)
ES-335S: See 335-S.
ES-335 Showcase Edition (Apr. 1988
    guitar of the month)
ES-335 Studio (1986–91), ES-Studio
    (1991)

ES-336 (1996–98) / CS-336
    (2002–current)

ES-340TD (1969–73)

ES-345TD (1959–82) (2002) / ES-345
    Reissue (2003–current)

ES-346 (1997–98) / Paul Jackson Jr
    ES-346 (1999–2006)

ES-347TD (1978–85) / ES-347S
    (1987–93)

ES-350 (also ES-350 Premier)
    (1947–56)
ES-350T (1955–63, 1977–80,
    1992–93, 1998–99)
ES-350T Centennial (Mar. 1994 guitar
    of the month)

ES-355TD (1958–71, 1994, 1997, 2004)
ES-355 Centennial (June 1994 guitar
    of the month)

ES-357 (1983–84)

ES-369 (1982)

ES-446s (2003–04)

ES-775 Classic Beauty (1990–93)

ES-Artist (1979–85)

ES-Studio: See ES-335.

ES Artist Signature models
Larry Carlton ES-335 (2002–current)
Eric Clapton ES-335 (2005)
Herb Ellis Signature ES-165
    (1991–2004)
Herb Ellis Signature ES-165 Plus
    (2002–04)
Steve Howe Signature ES-175
    (2001–current)
Paul Jackson Jr ES-346:
    See ES-346

Alvin Lee "Big Red" ES-335
(2005–current)
Lee Roy Parnell CS-336 (2004)
Andy Summers 1960 ES-335 (2001)

EXPLORER MODELS

Explorer (1958–59, 1975–79) /
Explorer I (1981–82) / Explorer 83
(1983) / Explorer (1984–89) /
Explorer Reissue (1990) / Explorer
'76 (1991–2003) / X-Plorer
(2003–current)

Explorer Black Hardware (1985)
Explorer Centennial (Apr. 1994 guitar
of the month)
Explorer CM: See The Explorer.
Explorer Gothic (1998–2001) /
X-Plorer Gothic (2001)
Explorer Heritage (1983)
Explorer Korina (1982–84)
Explorer Left Hand (1984–87)
Mahogany Explorer (2002–03)
Mahogany Explorer Split Headstock
(2003–04)
X-plorer New Century (2006–current)
Explorer Satin Finish (2003–04)
Explorer Synthesizer (1985)
Explorer Voodoo (2002–04)

Explorer II (1979–83)
Explorer III (1984–85)
Explorer III Black Hardware (1985)

Explorer 90 (1988)
Explorer 90 Double (1989–90)

Explorer Pro (2002–05, 2007–current)

The Explorer / Explorer CM (1976,
1981–84)

Explorer 400/400+ (1985–86)

X-plorer Studio (2004)

1958 Korina Explorer (1993–current)

Explorer Artist Signature models

Allen Collins Explorer (2003)

FIREBIRD MODELS

Firebird (1980)
Firebird I, reverse-body (1963–65,
1991–92) / 1963 Firebird I
(2000–current)
Firebird I, non-reverse (1965–69)
Firebird II (1981–82)
Firebird III, reverse-body (1963–65) /
1964 Firebird III (2000–current)
Firebird III, non-reverse (1965–69)
Firebird V, reverse-body (1963–65,
1986–87) / Firebird Reissue (1990)
/ Firebird V (1991–current) / 1964
Firebird V (Custom Shop,
2000–current)
Firebird V Celebrity Series (1991–93)
Firebird (V) (1972–73)
Firebird V, non-reverse (1965–69)
Firebird V 12-string (1966–67)
Firebird VII, reverse-body (1963–65,
1991–93, 2003–current) / 1965
Firebird VII (Custom Shop
2000–current)
Firebird VII Centennial (Sept. 1994
guitar of the month)

Firebird VII, non-reverse (1965–69)
Firebird VII non-reverse (2003–04)

Firebird 76 (1976–78)
Firebird Reissue: See Firebird V.
Firebird Studio (2004–current)
Non-reverse Firebird (2002–04)
Non-reverse Firebird Plus (2002)

FLYING V MODELS

Flying V (1958–59, 1965–69,
1971–79, 1984–89 / Flying V I
(1981–82) / Flying V 83 (1983) /
Flying V Reissue (1990) / Flying V
'67 (1991–2003) / X-Factor V
(2003–current)

Flying V II (1979–82)

Flying V '98 (1998)
Flying V '98 Gothic (1998–2001)
Flying V 400/400+ (1985–86)
Flying V Black Hardware (1985)
Flying V Centennial (July 1994 guitar
of the month)
Flying V Standard Quilt Top
(2004–06)
Flying V Custom (2002, 2004)
Flying V FF 8 (1981)
Flying V Heritage (1981–82)
Flying V Korina (1983)
Flying V Left Hand (1984–87)
Mahogany Flying V (2002–04)
Flying V Mirror Pickguard (2002)
Flying V Primavera (1994)
Flying V Voodoo (2002)
Flying V XPL (1984–86)
Flying V XPL Black Hardware (1985)

X-Factor V Faded (2003–current)

X-Factor V New Century
(2006–current)

Flying V 90 (1988)

Flying V 90 Double (1989–90)

Flying V CMT / The V (1981–85)

1958 Korina Flying V (1991–current) /
1959 Korina Flying V
(1994–current)

Flying V Artist Signature models

Jimi Hendrix '69 Flying V Custom
(1991–1993)

Jimi Hendrix Psychedelic Flying V
(2006)

Judas Priest Flying V (2005–current)

Lenny Kravitz 1967 Flying V
(2001–04)

Lonnie Mack Flying V (1993–94)

LES PAUL MODELS

Les Paul Acoustic (2001–02) / Les
Paul Acoustic Plain-top (2003–05)

Les Paul Active: See L.P. Artist

Les Paul Anniversary (1992–93)

Les Paul Artisan (1976–1981)

Les Paul Artist: See L.P. Artist

Les Paul Bantam Elite (1995) / Les
Paul Florentine Standard

(1995–1997)

Les Paul Bantam Elite Plus (1995) /
Les Paul Florentine Standard Plus
(1995–1998)

Les Paul Elite Diamond Sparkle
(1995–97)

Les Paul Baritone: See Les Paul
Studio Baritone.

Les Paul BFG (2007–current)

Les Paul Black Beauty: See Les Paul
Custom.

Les Paul Catalina (1996–97)

Les Paul Class 5 (2001–current)

Les Paul Classic (1990–current)

Les Paul Classic Antique
(2007–current)

Les Paul Classic Birdseye (1993)

Les Paul Classic Celebrity Series
(July 1991)

Les Paul Classic Centennial
(Feb. 1994 guitar of the month)

Les Paul Classic Custom
(2007–current)

Les Paul Classic Mahogany Top
(2000)

Les Paul Classic Plus (1991–96,
1999–current)

Les Paul Classic Premium Plus
(1993–97)

Les Paul Classic M-III electronics
(1991–93)

Les Paul CMT (1986–mid 1989)

Les Paul Custom (late 1953–63,
1968–current)

Les Paul '57 Black Beauty 3-Pickup
Centennial (Nov. 1994 guitar of the
month) Les Paul Black Beauty '82
(1982–83)

Les Paul Custom/3 pickups
(1971–73, 1976, 1978)

Les Paul Custom 20th Anniversary
(1974)

Les Paul Custom 25th Anniversary
(1977)

Les Paul Custom 35th Anniversary
(1989)

Les Paul Custom '54 (1972)

Les Paul Custom/400 (1991–92)

Les Paul Custom Black Beauty '54
Reissue (1991–current)

Les Paul Custom Black Beauty '57
Reissue (1991–current)

Les Paul Custom/maple fingerboard
(1975–81)

Les Paul Custom/nickel-plated parts
(1976, 1979–86, 1996)

Les Paul Custom Plus (1991–97)

Les Paul Custom Showcase Edition
(Mar. 1988 guitar of the month)

Les Paul Mahogany Custom (1997)

Les Paul Super Custom (1984)

10th Anniversary '68 Les Paul
Custom (2003)

Les Paul Custom Lite (1987–89)

Les Paul Custom Lite Showcase
Edition (Aug. 1988 guitar of the
month)

Les Paul DC Pro (1997–98, 2006–current)
Les Paul DC Studio (1997–98)
Les Paul DC Standard (Les Paul Standard-DC) (1998)

Les Paul Standard Doublecut Plus (2001–current)
Les Paul Standard Doublecut w/P-90s (2003–05)

Les Paul Deluxe (1969–85, 1992)
Les Paul Deluxe BB (1975–77)
Les Paul Deluxe Hall of Fame Edition (1991)
Les Paul Deluxe RR (1975)
30th Anniversary Les Paul Deluxe (2000)

Les Paul Diamond (2003–05)

Les Paul Double-Cutaway (various models): also see Les Paul DC, Les Paul Faded Doublecut.
Les Paul Double-Cutaway XPL (1984–86)
Les Paul Double-Cutaway XPL/400 (1984)

Les Paul Elegant (1996–current)
Les Paul Elegant Quilt (1997)
Les Paul Elegant Double Quilt (1997)
Les Paul Elegant Super Double Quilt (1997)

Les Paul Elite: See Les Paul Bantam Elite.

Les Paul Faded Doublecut (2003–current)

Les Paul Flame (2003–05)
Les Paul Flametop: See Les Paul Reissue.

Les Paul Florentine: See Les Paul Bantam Elite.

Les Paul Gothic: See Les Paul Studio Gothic.

Les Paul GT (2006)

Les Paul Goddess (2006–current)

Les Paul HD.X6-Pro Digital (2007–current)

Les Paul Heritage 80 (1980–82)
Les Paul Heritage 80 Elite (1980–82)
Les Paul Heritage 80 Award

Les Paul Jumbo (1969–71)

Les Paul Junior (1954–63, 1986–92) (2001–02)

1957 Les Paul Jr Double Cutaway (1998–99)
1957 Les Paul Jr Single Cutaway (1998–current)
1958 Les Paul Jr Double Cutaway (2000–current)
Les Paul Junior ¾-scale (1956–61)
Les Paul Junior II (1989)
Les Paul Jr DC SP: See Les Paul Special Double Cutaway.
Les Paul Jr Double Cutaway (1987–92, 1995)
Les Paul Jr Double Cutaway Special: See Les Paul Specials.

Les Paul Junior Lite (1999–2002)
Les Paul Jr Pro: See Junior Pro.
Les Paul Junior Special: See Les Paul Special.
Les Paul Junior TV: See Les Paul TV.

Les Paul K-II (1980)

Les Paul Kalamazoo (1979)

Les Paul Korina (1997)

Les Paul Mahogany (1993)

Les Paul Melody Maker (2007–current)

Les Paul Menace (2006–current)

Les Paul Model: See Les Paul Standard.

Les Paul New Century: See Les Paul Special.

Les Paul North Star (1978)

Les Paul Personal (1969–70)

Les Paul Pro-Deluxe (1978–81)

Les Paul Pro Showcase Edition (Dec. 1988 guitar of the month)

Les Paul Professional (1969–70)

Les Paul Recording (1971–79)

Les Paul Reissue (1983–1991) / Les Paul '59 Flametop Reissue

(1991–current) / **Les Paul '60 Flametop Reissue** (1991–current)

'52 Les Paul Gold-top Aged (2002)
'54 Les Paul Gold-top Reissue (1996–current)
'54 Les Paul Oxblood (1997–2003)
'56 Les Paul Gold-top Reissue (1991–current)
'57 LP Gold-top (1993–current)
'57 LP Gold-top Darkback Reissue (2000–current)
'57 Les Paul Gold-top Mary Ford (1997–current)
'58 Les Paul Figured Top (1996–99, 2001–03)
'58 Les Paul Plain-top (1994–99, 2003–current)
Guitar Trader Reissue (1982–c1985)
Leo's Reissue (1982–c1985)
Les Paul Reissue Gold-top (1983–91)
Strings and Things Reissue (1975–78)
Jimmy Wallace Reissue (1978–97)

Les Paul Session: See L.P. Session.

Les Paul/SG '61 Reissue: See SG Reissue.

Les Paul/SG: See SG Custom, SG Special, SG Standard.

Les Paul Signature (1973–77)

Les Paul Silver Streak (1982)

Les Paul SM (1980)

Les Paul Smartwood Exotic

(1998–2002)
Les Paul Smartwood (Standard) (1996–99)
Les Paul Smartwood Studio (2003–current)

Les Paul Special (1955–59) (1989–97)

Also see Les Paul Junior listing for Specials with such model names as "Junior LIte" or "Junior II"
Les Paul Jr Double Cutaway Special (1988)
Les Paul Jr Special (1999–2001)
Les Paul Junior Special Plus (2001–05)
1960 Les Paul Special Single Cutaway (1998–current)
1960 Les Paul Special Double Cutaway (1998–current): 2 black soapbar P-90 pickups, Vintage Original Spec aging treatment optional from 2006.
Les Paul Special ¾-scale (1959–63): 22¾-inch scale, 15 frets clear of body. Production: 51 (1954–60).
Les Paul Special 400 (1985)
Les Paul Special Double CMT (1979)
Les Paul Special Double Cutaway (1976, 1978–85, 1993–94)
Les Paul Special Double Cut Centennial (Jan. 1994 guitar of the month)
Les Paul Special New Century (2006–current)
Les Paul Special Single Cutaway Centennial (1994)
Les Paul Special SL (Sans Lacquer) (1998)

Les Paul Spotlight Special (1983–84)

Les Paul Standard (1958–63, 1968–69, 1972–current) / **Les Paul Model** (1952–57)

Les Paul Custom Shop Standard (1997–98)
Les Paul Standard '58 (1971–73)
Les Paul Standard 82 (1980–82)
Les Paul Standard 83 (1983)
Les Paul Standard Birdseye (1993–96)
Les Paul Standard Centennial (Oct. 1994 guitar of the month)
Les Paul Standard-DC, Standard Double-Cut, Standard Double-Cut Plus: See Les Paul DC Standard.
Les Paul Standard Faded (2005–current)
Les Paul Standard Limited Edition (2007)
Les Paul Standard P-100 (1989)
Les Paul Standard Plus (1995–97)
Les Paul Standard Premium Plus (2002–current)
Les Paul Standard Raw Power (2000–2001)
Les Paul Standard Showcase Edition (June 1988)
Les Paul Standard Sparkle Top (2000)
Les Paul Standard Special (1983)

Les Paul Standard Lite (1999–current)

Les Paul Standard reissues: See Les Paul Reissue

a-z

Les Paul Studio (1983–current)

Les Paul Smartwood Studio: See Les Paul Smartwood.

Les Paul Swamp Ash Studio (2003–current)

Les Paul Studio Baritone (2004–05)

Les Paul Studio Custom (1984–85)

Les Paul Studio Gem (1996–97)

Les Paul Studio Gothic (2000–01)

Les Paul Studio Premium Plus (2006–current)

Les Paul Studio Standard (1984–87)

Les Paul Studio Synthesizer (1985)

Les Paul Studio Lite (1987–98)

Les Paul Studio Lite/lightly figured maple top (1991)

Les Paul Studio Lite/M-III electronics (1991–94)

Les Paul Supreme (2003–current)

Les Paul Tie-Dye (1996)

Les Paul TV (1954–59)

Les Paul Ultima (1996–current)

Les Paul Vixen (2006–current)

Les Paul Voodoo (2002–04)

Les Paul XPL (1984)

Les Paul XR: See L.P. XR.

Les Paul 25th Anniversary (1978–79)

Les Paul 30th Anniversary (1982–83)

Les Paul 55 (1974–80)

L.P. Artist (Les Paul Artist, Les Paul Active) (1979–81)

L.P. Session (L.P. XR-III): No information unavailable.

L.P. XR-1 (1981–82)

L.P. XR-II (1981–82)

L.P. XR-III (1982)

Old Hickory Les Paul (1998)

The Les Paul (1976–79)

The Paul II (1996–97) / The Paul II SL (Sans Lacquer) (1998)

The Paul (Standard) (1978–81) / Firebrand Les Paul (1981)

The Paul Deluxe (1980–85)

Les Paul Artist Signature models

(2 humbuckers and 4 knobs unless otherwise noted)

Duane Allman (2003)

Billy Jo Armstrong Les Paul Junior (2006–current)

Dickey Betts '57 Redtop Les Paul (2002–03)

Dickey Betts Ultra Aged 1957 Les Paul Gold-top (2001–2003)

Peter Frampton Les Paul (2000–current)

Ace Frehley Les Paul (1997–2001)

Warren Haynes '58 Les Paul (2006)

Bob Marley Les Paul Special (2002–03)

Gary Moore Les Paul (2000–01)

Jimmy Page Les Paul, 1st version (1995–99)

Jimmy Page Les Paul, 2nd version (2004–current)

Joe Perry Les Paul (1996–2000)

Joe Perry Boneyard Les Paul (2003–current)

Gary Rossington Les Paul (2002)

Neal Schon Les Paul (2005–current)

Slash Les Paul (1997)

Slash Les Paul Signature (2004–current)

John Sykes Les Paul Custom (2007)

Pete Townshend Les Paul Deluxe #9 (2006)

Pete Townshend Deluxe (2006)

Pete Townshend Deluxe Gold-top (2006)

Zakk Wylde Bullseye Les Paul (2000–current)

Zakk Wylde Camo Bullseye Les Paul (2004–current)

Zakk Wylde Rough Top Les Paul (2000–02)

Zakk Wylde Custom (Bottle Cap) (1999, 2002)

SG MODELS

SG Artist (1981) / SG-R1 (1980)

SG Classic (1999–2001)

SG Custom (1963–79) / SG '62 Custom (1986) / SG Les Paul Custom (1987–90) / Les Paul/SG

Custom Reissue (1997–2005) / **SG Custom** (2006–current)

Les Paul SG '67 Custom (1992–1993)

SG Custom Showcase Edition (October 1988)

10th Anniversary SG Custom (2003–04)

30th Anniversary SG Custom (1991)

1967 SG Custom (1991)

SG Deluxe (1971–72, 1981–84, 1998–2000)

SG Elegant Quilt Top (2004–06)

SG Elite (1987–89)

SG Exclusive (1979)

SG Goddess (2006–current)

SG Gothic: See SG Special Gothic.

SG GT (2006–current)

SG Junior (1963–70, 1991–93)

SG-100 Junior: See SG-100.

SG Les Paul (Les Paul with SG body): See Les Paul Custom, Les Paul Junior, Les Paul Standard, Les Paul/SG.

SG Menace (2006–current)

SG Pro (1971, 1973–74)

SG Reissue (1986–87) / **SG '62 Reissue** (1988–90) / **Les Paul SG '61 Reissue** (1993–97) / **SG '61 Reissue** (1998–current) (also see Les Paul/SG Standard Reissue)

SG Select (2007–current)

SG Special (1959–70, 1972–78, 1985–current) / **Gibson Special** (1985)

Generation Swine SG Special (mid 1997)

Les Paul/SG Special Reissue (2001–03) / **SG Special** (Custom Shop version 2004–current)

SG Special ¾-scale (1959–61)

SG Special Faded (2002–current)

SG Special Faded 3 Pickup (2007–current)

SG Special Gothic (1999–2000) / **SG Gothic** (2001–02)

SG Special New Century (2006–current)

SG Special Reissue (2004–current)

SG Standard (1963–70 1972–80 1983–86 1988–current) (also see SG Reissue, The SG)

Les Paul/SG Standard Reissue (2001–03) / **SG Standard** (Custom shop version 2004–current)

SG '62 Showcase Edition (Apr. 1988 guitar of the month)

SG/Les Paul with Deluxe Lyre Vibrato (2000–2002)

SG Standard Celebrity Series (Aug. 1991)

SG Standard Korina (1993–94)

SG Studio (1978)

SG Supreme (1999–2004 2007–current) / **SG Supreme '57 Humbucker** (2005–2006)

SG TV (1960–67)

SG Voodoo (2002–04)

SG-X: See All American I.

SG-Z (1998)

SG I (1972–73)

SG I with Junior pickup (1972)

SG II (1972)

SG III with humbuckers (1975)

SG III (1972–73)

SG-3 (2007–current)

SG '61 Reissue, SG '62 Reissue: See SG Standard.

SG '62 Showcase Edition: See SG Standard.

SG 90 Single (1988–90)

SG 90 Double (1988–90)

SG-100 (1971)

SG-100 Junior (1972)

SG-200 (1971)

SG-250 (1971)

SG 400 (1985–86)

The SG (1979–80) / **SG Standard** (1981)

The SG / The SG Deluxe (1979–84)

SG Artist Signature models

Elliot Easton Custom SG (2007–current)

Tony Iommi Les Paul SG (1998, 2001–05)

Judas Priest SG (2005–current)
Gary Rossington SG (2003)
Pete Townsend Ltd Edition SG
   Special (2000)
Pete Townsend Signature SG Special
   (2001)
Angus Young Signature SG
   (2000–current)

OTHER MODELS

All American I (1995–97) / SG-X
   (1998–2000)
All American II (1995–97)

Alpha Series: See Q-100.

Black Beauty: See Les Paul Custom.

Black Knight Custom (1984)

BluesHawk (1996–2003)

Byrdland (1955–current)
Byrdland Florentine (1998–current)

CF-100E (1951–58)

Challenger I (1983–84)
Challenger II (1983–84)

Citation (1969–70, 1975, 1979–83,
   1993–current)

Corvette: See Custom models.

Corvus I (1982–84)

Corvus II (1982–84)

Corvus III (1982–84)
Crest (1969–71)
Crest Special (1961–63, 1969)

CS-336, CS-346: See ES-336, ES-346

CS-356 (2003–current)
10th Anniversary CS-356
   (2003–2004)

Doubleneck: any combination of
   necks was available by custom
   order from 1958–69. For regular
   production models see EDS-1275,
   EMS-1235, EBS-1250.

EBSF-1250 (1962–68)

EDS-1275 Double 12 (1958–68,
   1974–current)
EDS-1275 Centennial (May 1994
   guitar of the month)
Jimmy Page Double Neck (2007)
EDS custom: Any combination of
   guitar, bass, mandolin or banjo
   necks was available by custom
   order.

EMS-1235 Double Mandolin
   (1958–68)
EMS custom: Any combination of
   guitar, bass, mandolin or banjo
   necks was available by custom
   order.

EXP 425 (1985–86)

Firebrand: See The SG, The Paul,
   335-S

Futura (1982–84)
Futura Reissue (1996) / Mahogany
   Futura (2002–04)

GGC-700 (1981–82)

GK-55 (1979–80)

Guitar Trader Reissue: See Les Paul
   Standard Reissue.

KZ-II (1980–81)

Invader (1983–88, prototypes from
   1980)

Graceland (1995–96)

J-160E (1954–78, 1990–96) / J-160
   Standard (2002) / J-160 VS
   Standard (2002, 2005–current)
J-160E Montana Special (1995)
J-160E Yamano Reissue (1996)

J-190EC Super Fusion (2001–04)

Junior Pro (1988)

Kalamazoo Award (1978–84)

Kalamazoo Award 100th Anniversary
   (1991)

L-4CES (1958, 1969, 1986–2003) /
   L-4CES Mahogany (2004–06)

10th Anniversary L-4 Thinline (2003)
L-5CES (1951–current)
L-5CES Centennial (Dec. 1994 guitar
   of the month)

L-5 CEST (1954–62, 1983)
L-5 Custom: See Super V
L-5S (1973–84)
L-5 Signature (2001–05)
L-5 Studio (1996–current)

L-6S/L6-S Custom: (1973–75 L-6S;
    1975–79 L-6S Custom)
L-6S Deluxe (1975–80)

Landmark (1996–97)

Le Grand: See Johnny Smith Artist
    Signature model.

Leo's Reissue: See Les Paul Standard
    Reissue.

Little Lucille: See B.B. King Artist
    Signature model.

The Log (2003)

Lucille, Lucille Standard: See B.B.
    King Artist Signature model.

M-III Standard (1991–95)
M-III (1996–97)
M-III Deluxe (1991–92)
M-III-H (Standard) (1991–92)
M-III-H Deluxe (1991)
M-III Standard (1991–95)
M-III Stealth (1991)
M-IV S Standard (1993–95)
M-IV S Deluxe (1993–95)

Mach II: See U-2.
Map-shape (1983)

Marauder (1975–81)

Marauder Custom (1976–77)

Melody Maker / MM (1959–70,
    1986–92)

MM ¾-scale (1959–70)
MM-D/Melody Maker Double 1st
    version (1960–70, 1976)
Melody Maker Double 2nd version
    (1977–83)
MM-III (1967–71)
MM-12 (1967–71)

Midnight Special (1974–79)

MM: See Melody Maker.

Moderne Heritage (1982–83)

MV-2, MV-II, MV-10, MV-X: See Victory

Nighthawk Custom (1993–98)
Nighthawk Special (1993–98)
Nighthawk Standard (1993–98)

Pioneer Cutaway (2004–current)

Q-100 (Alpha Series) (1985)
Q-200 (1985)
Q-300/Q-3000 (1985)
Q-4000 (1985) / 400 (1986)

Ranger (2004–current)

RD: See RD Artist.
RD Custom (1977–78) / 77 Custom
    (1979)
RD Standard (1977–1978)
RD Artist/79 (1979–80) / RD (1981)
RD Artist/77 (1980): 25½-inch scale.

RD Artist CMT (1981)

S-1 (1976–79)

Sonex-180 (1980) / Sonex-180
    Deluxe (1981–83)
Sonex-180 Deluxe Left Hand (1982)
Sonex-180 Custom (1980–82)
Sonex Artist (1981–84)

Special I (1983–85)
Special II (1983–85)

Spiderman: See Custom models, Web
    Slinger One.

Spirit I: (1982–87)
Spirit I XPL (1985–86)
Spirit II (1982–87)
Spirit II XPL (1985–86)

SR-71 (1987–89)

Strings and Things Reissue: See Les
    Paul Reissue.

Super V CES (1978–92) / L-5CES
    Custom (1973–77)
Super V/BJB (1978–83): 1 floating
    pickup. Production: 43 (1979).

Super 300CES (1954)

Super 400CES (1951–current)
Super 400C 50th Anniversary (1984)

Switchmaster: See ES-5
    Switchmaster.

TF-7: See Tal Farlow Artist Sig. model.

The Explorer: See Explorer models.

The Hawk (1996–97)

The Les Paul: See Les Paul models.

The SG: See SG models.

The V: See Flying V CMT.

Traveling Songwriter (2005–current)

U-2/Mach II (1987–90)
U-2 Showcase Edition (Nov. 1988 guitar of the month)

US-1: (1986–90)

V-Factor X: See Flying V.

Vegas High Roller (2006–current)
Vegas Standard (2006–current)

Victory MV-2 or **MV-II** (1981–84)
Victory MV-10 or **MV-X** (1981–84)

Jimmy Wallace Reissue: See Les Paul Standard Reissue.

WRC (1987–89)
WRC Showcase Edition (Sept. 1988 guitar of the month)

X-Factor V: See Flying V Reissue.

X-Plorer: See Explorer Reissue.

XPL Custom (1985–86)
XPL Standard (1985)

77 Custom: See RD Custom.

335-S Deluxe (1980–82)

335-S Custom (1980)
335-S Standard (1980)

1275: See EDS-1275.

Other Artist Signature models

Johnny A. Signature (2003–current)

Tom DeLonge Signature (2003–current)

Duane Eddy Signature (2005–current)

Tal Farlow Signature (1962–67, 1993–current)
TF-7 (1991)

Barney Kessel Custom (1961–73)
Barney Kessel Regular (1961–73)

B.B. King Standard (1980) / **Lucille Standard** (1981–85)
B.B. King Custom (1980) / **Lucille** (1981–85) / **B.B. King Lucille** (1986–current)
B.B. King "Little Lucille" (1999–current)

John Lennon J-160E Bed-In (1998)
John Lennon J-160E Fab Four (1998)
John Lennon J-160E Magical Tour (1998)
John Lennon J-160E Peace (2002)

Trini Lopez Signature Deluxe (1964–71)
Trini Lopez Signature Standard (1964–71)

Pat Martino Custom / Pat Martino Signature (1999–2006)
Pat Martino Standard (1999–2000)

Wes Montgomery Signature (1993–current)
Wes Montgomery Heart (1997)

Jimmy Page EDS-1275 Double Neck (2007)

Lee Ritenour L-5 Signature (2003–current)

Howard Roberts Custom (1970, 1974–80)
Howard Roberts Artist (1976–80)
Howard Roberts Artist Double Pickup (1979–80)
Howard Roberts DE (1970)
Howard Roberts Standard Electric (1970)
Howard Roberts Fusion (1979–1990) / **Howard Roberts Fusion II** (1988–90) / **Howard Roberts Fusion III** (1991–current)

Johnny Smith (1961–88) / **Chet Atkins (JS) Double** (1989–91) / **Le Grand** (1993–current)
Johnny Smith Double (1963–89)

a–z

CUSTOM MODELS
Product or personality themes

Les Paul '60 Corvette (1995–97)

Les Paul '63 Corvette Sting Ray
(1995–97)

Jim Beam Les Paul (2000–03)

Chevrolet SSR (2003)

Copperhead SG (2003)

Crazy Horse Les Paul (2003)

Dale Earnhardt Les Paul (1999–2001)

Dale Earnhardt "The Intimidator"
Les Paul (2000–01)

Dale Earnhardt Jr Les Paul (2001)

Hummer Les Paul (2003–04)

Indian Chief Les Paul (2002)

Playboy 2001 Playmate of the Year
(2001)

Playboy Hottie SG (2003–04)

Playboy CS-356 (2003–04)

Playboy Rabbit Head CS-356
(2003–04)

Kiefer Sutherland KS-336
(2007–current)

Web-Slinger One (1999)

X-Men Wolverine Les Paul
(2001)

50th Anniversary Les Paul Corvette
(2003)

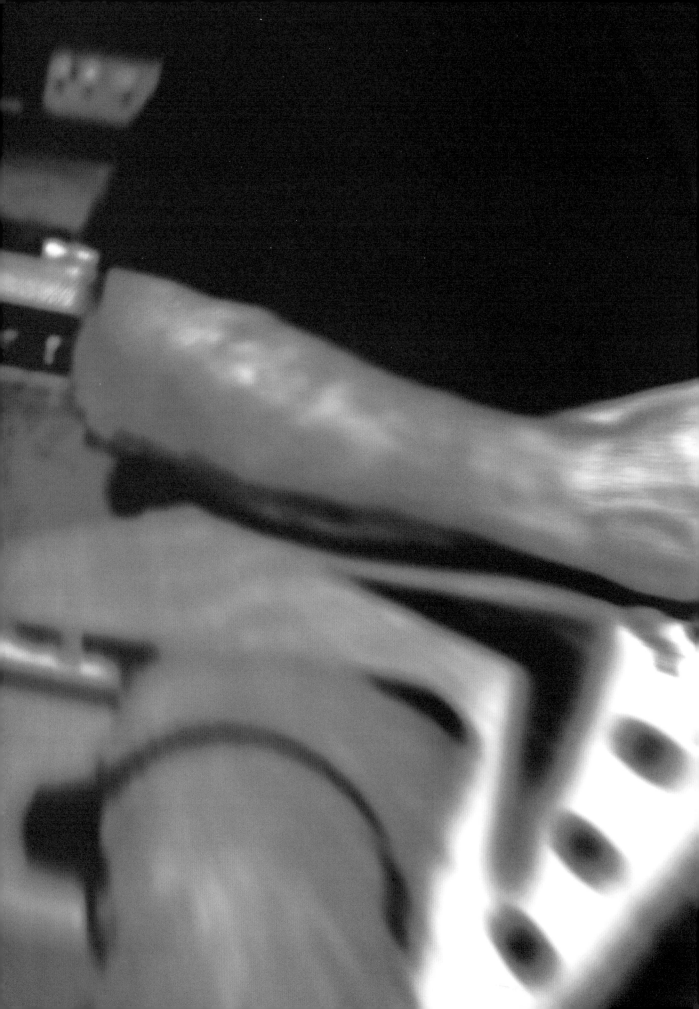

models: year-by-year

This listing shows in chronological order the production-model electric guitars manufactured by Gibson between 1936 and 2007. Basic specifications are included for each model. The start date shown is the year that production commenced for each. Production numbers are included for models where available, although records are not consistent for the entire history of Gibson guitar production. Where included, these have been taken from the personal records of Gibson employee Julius Bellson for the pre-World War II years (1937–41) and from Gibson shipping totals (1948–79).

Format of the model listings:

Model name (years of production) / **Later model name** (years of production)
Quick identification keys
- Body & Hardware specifications
- Neck specifications
- Pickups & Controls specifications
Production numbers (not all years and models available)

Related models (in alphabetical order), production years, specs and production numbers

1936

ES-150 pre-WWII (1936–42)
Non-cut archtop, dot inlays, pearl logo
- **Body & Hardware:** full-depth hollowbody, 16¼-inch wide, X-braced carved spruce top, flat back (arched from 1940), single-bound top and back, single-bound pickguard, Sunburst finish.
- **Neck:** single-bound rosewood fingerboard (unbound from 1940), dot inlays, pearl logo.
- **Pickups & Controls:** "Charlie Christian" blade pickup in hexagonal housing (rectangular metal-

covered with screw-poles from 1940), single-ply binding around pickup and around blade (triple-ply 1938–9), 2 knobs, jack at tailpiece base.
Production: 1,629 (1937–41).

1937

EST-150 (1937–39) / **ETG-150** (1940–42): Tenor neck, arched back, jack on side.
Production: 95 (1937–41).

1938

ES-100 (1938–41)/ **ES-125** pre-WWII (1941–43)
Non-cut archtop, 1 pickup, prewar script logo in paint
- **Body & Hardware:** full-depth hollowbody, 14¼-inch wide, X-braced carved spruce top, maple back and sides, flat back (arched from 1940), single-bound top and back, Sunburst finish.
- **Neck:** unbound rosewood fingerboard (unbound from 1940), dot inlays, silkscreen logo.
- **Pickups & Controls:** blade pickup with white rectangular housing (rectangular metal-covered with screw-poles from 1940), pickup in neck position (bridge position from 1940), 2 knobs, jack on side.
Production: 585 (ES-100); 152 (ES-125, 1941).

1939

ESP-150 (1939): Plectrum neck, arched back, jack on side.
Production: 1.

ES-250 (1939–40)
Non-cut archtop, open-book inlays, Charlie Christian pickup
- **Body & Hardware:** 17-inch wide, carved spruce top, maple sides and arched back, triple-bound

THE BIRTH OF THE GIBSON ELECTRIC GUITAR

Working alone in his back-room workshop in Kalamazoo, Michigan, Orville Gibson invented the archtop guitar in the 1890s. In the 1920s and early '30s this was the most popular type of 'Spanish' style guitar with players in dance bands, swing orchestras, and western swing outfits – in short, with the guitarists who were finding themselves most in need of amplification. The form had reached its zenith in many players' and collectors' eyes with the Lloyd Loar-designed L-5 of 1922, an elaborately crafted instrument with a laboriously hand-carved solid spruce top. Designed for optimum performance and tone, the L-5 also had pretty good volume for an acoustic archtop, and quickly became the epitome of its type; but laboring away at the back of a stage crowded with horns, a piano, a drummer, and more and more often a singer with a microphone connected to a PA system, the type of guitarist who could afford an L-5 was rapidly finding he needed something louder to cut it at many playing dates. Enter the electric guitar, and a new era in both the instrument and the music that it helped to make possible.

Gibson wasn't the first to experiment with amplifying the guitar, but it was the first established company to offer an electric guitar as a standard production model. In 1936, the revolutionary ES-150 'Electric Spanish' guitar hit the scene. It had a 16¼-inch body with a carved, X-braced spruce top, a flat maple back, simple dot position markers in the fingerboard, and, most crucially, a single 'blade'-style magnetic pickup mounted in the body of the guitar and positioned near the end of the fingerboard, along with volume and tone controls to govern it. Although outwardly it appears to be just another single-coil pickup, these early Gibson pickups – which have forever after been known as 'Charlie Christian pickups' because of their use by the formative jazz guitarist – actually consist of a long bar magnet suspended under the top of the guitar by three adjustment screws, which is attached to a single blade pole-piece that protrudes through the visible surround.

Although rather basic, even crude by today's standards, the ES-150 was a considerable success, and played a major part in ushering in the era of amplified music. It was a rather boomy, potentially bass-heavy sounding guitar, and prone to howling feedback if you weren't careful with volume levels and playing position, but it gave guitarists a means of escaping the ghetto of the rhythm section and even taking a spin in the spotlight now and then. This early bullseye gave Gibson the confidence to follow up with a succession of electric models in the prewar years, first looking down-market with the more affordable 14¼-inch ES-100 of 1938, then up-market with the 17-inch ES-250 of 1939. In 1940 the even more deluxe, 17-inch-wide ES-300 was introduced, which also boasted a carved, arched maple back. But it would be the last Gibson electric to hit the scene before World War II put a halt to guitar production.

'39

pickguard, large tailpiece, Sunburst or Natural finish.

- **Neck:** bound rosewood fingerboard, open-book inlay (some with double-parallelogram, some with fancy pattern in rectangular inserts), 2-piece maple neck with center stripe, stairstep headstock (some with non-stairstep, bound or unbound), stinger on back of headstock, pearl logo (some with post-WWII logo).
- **Pickups & Controls:** triple-bound Charlie Christian pickup with 6 blades (some assembled post-WWII with P-90 pickup), 2 knobs, jack at tailpiece base.

Production: 70.

1940

ES-300 pre-WWII (1940–42)

Non-cut archtop, double-parallelogram inlays, prewar logo

- **Body & Hardware:** 17-inch wide, parallel-braced carved spruce top, most with dowel supports under bridge, carved maple back, tailpiece with pointed ends and raised diamond and arrows, triple-bound top (some single-ply) and back, bound tortoiseshell celluloid pickguard.
- **Neck:** 2-piece maple neck with stripe down middle, double-parallelogram inlay, single-bound peghead, black "stinger" on back of peghead, crown peghead inlay (some with 7-piece split-diamond), pearl logo.
- **Pickups & Controls:** 7-inch slant-mounted oblong pickup with adjustable poles (4⅛-inch pickup from 1941), jack on side.

Production: 194 (1940–41).

1941–1944

Production suspended during World War II

1945

ES-300 post-WWII (1945–52)

Non-cut archtop, double-parallelogram inlays, postwar logo

- **Body & Hardware:** 17-inch laminated maple body (a few early with 5-ply mahogany body), trapeze tailpiece with pointed ends and 3 raised parallelograms (early with plate tailpiece with 2 *f*-hole cutouts), laminated beveled-edge pickguard (early with bound tortoiseshell celluloid pickguard), triple-bound top and back, Sunburst or Natural finish (a few black, 1945).
- **Neck:** 1-piece mahogany neck, bound rosewood fingerboard, double-parallelogram inlay, bound

peghead, crown peghead inlay, plastic keystone tuner buttons: mid 1946.

- **Pickups & Controls:** P-90 pickup in neck position (2 pickups from 1948), 2 knobs (master tone knob added on upper treble bout, 1948).

Production: 826 (1948–56).

1946

ES-125 post-WWII (1946–70)

Non-cut archtop, 1 P-90 pickup, postwar logo, dot or trapezoid inlays

- **Body & Hardware:** 16½-inch full-depth hollowbody of laminated maple (some with all-mahogany body), tortoise pickguard, trapeze tailpiece, single-bound top and back, Sunburst finish.
- **Neck:** unbound rosewood fingerboard (unbound from 1940), pearloid trapezoid inlay (some with dot inlay from 1946, all with dot inlay from 1950), decal logo.
- **Pickups & Controls:** P-90 pickup in neck position (earliest with no non-adjustable poles or no poles), 2 knobs.

Production: 32,940.

1947–48

ES-150 post-WWII (1947–56)

Non-cut archtop, 17-inch wide, single P-90 pickup, dot or trapezoid inlays

- **Body & Hardware:** full-depth laminated maple hollowbody, 17-inch wide, laminated beveled-edge pickguard, bound top and back.
- **Neck:** unbound rosewood fingerboard (bound from 1950), dot inlay (trapezoid from 1950), silkscreen logo.
- **Pickups & Controls:** P-90 pickup in neck position, jack on side.

Production: 3,447 (1948–56).

LAMINATED WOODS FOR SOLID TONES: THE ES-175

Having returned to the market with the ES-300, ES-125, ES-150 and ES-350 following the war, Gibson was already envisioning a future that took the electrified instrument a step further away from the constructional standards for quality acoustic archtop guitars. All of these models were still being made with carved solid-spruce tops. Gibson soon deduced, however, that once a guitar is amplified past its acoustic volume, considerations of acoustic tone take a back seat to amplified performance, and that amplified performance could be improved – arguably – with the use of a stiffer laminated top. Using laminated wood would also ease production and reduce expense, since the top could be pressed into its arched shape, rather than painstakingly carved by hand. The result was the ES-175, released in 1949 – Gibson's first archtop with a laminated maple top, and also the first with a pointed cutaway.

The model was born with a single P-90 pickup in the neck position, single volume and tone controls, and a body that was 16¼ inches wide and 3¼ inches deep. Two pickups were available from 1951. Gibson's hopes for the instrument bore fruit: the ES-175 was a little punchier and more cutting than traditional electric archtops, and also somewhat (if only slightly) more resistant to feedback. It quickly became a standard for many jazz players, and kicked off a line of laminated-wood electric archtops that remains popular to this day.

Not that Gibson was giving up on the carved-top archtop electric. In 1949 the company also introduced the ES-5, an upmarket model with 17-inch-wide body with rounded cutaway and – another first in the electric guitar world – three P-90 pickups (the model was modified into the ES-5 Switchmaster in 1955 to improve the selection facilities for these pickups). Gibson further reaffirmed its commitment to upscale archtop electrics with the introduction of the L-5CES and Super 400CES in 1951, but in the years to follow the laminated models would prove to be the greater popular success across the full range of electric guitar genres.

ETG-150 (1947–71): Tenor neck, electric version of TG-50 acoustic, 16¼-inch hollowbody, 1 P-90 pickup, laminated beveled-edge pickguard, bound fingerboard, dot inlays, no peghead ornament. Production: 476 (1948–60).

ES-350 (also **ES-350 Premier**) (1947–56)
Single-cut archtop, rounded horn, double-parallelogram inlays
- **Body & Hardware:** 17-inch wide, rosewood bridge (Tune-o-matic 1956), trapeze tailpiece with pointed ends and 3 raised parallelograms, laminated beveled-edge pickguard (early with bound tortoiseshell celluloid pickguard), triple-bound top and back, gold-plated hardware, Sunburst or Natural finish.

- **Neck:** 2-piece maple neck with stripe down center, single-bound fingerboard, double-parallelogram inlay, single-bound peghead, black "stinger" on back of peghead, crown peghead inlay crown peghead inlay, plastic keystone tuner buttons.
- **Pickups & Controls:** 1 P-90 pickup (2 pickups from 1948), 2 knobs (master tone control added on cutaway from 1948, 4 knobs and toggle switch from 1952).
Production: 1,056 (1948–56).

1949

ES-5 (1949–55)
Single-cut archtop, 3 pickups, 4 knobs

- **Body & Hardware:** 17-inch wide, rounded cutaway, rosewood bridge (Tune-o-matic from 1955) trapeze tailpiece with pointed ends and 3 raised parallelograms, laminated beveled-edge pickguard, triple-bound top and back (5-ply from 1955), bound *f*-holes (a few early unbound), gold-plated hardware, Sunburst or Natural finish.
- **Neck:** 2-piece maple neck with stripe down center, pointed-end rosewood fingerboard with 5-ply binding, large pearl block inlays, single-bound peghead, black "stinger" on back of peghead, crown peghead inlay.
- **Pickups & Controls:** 3 P-90 pickups (Alnico V specified, 1955), 3 volume controls, 1 master tone knob on cutaway bout.
Production: 911 (includes some ES-5 Switchmasters 1955).

ES-175 single pickup (1949–72)
Single-cut archtop, pointed horn, double-parallelogram inlay, 1 pickup
- **Body & Hardware:** 16½-inch wide, laminated maple body, pointed cutaway, laminated beveled-edge pickguard, rosewood bridge (Tune-o-matic from 1977), hinged tailpiece with pointed ends and 3 raised parallelograms (T-center with zigzag tubes 1958–71), triple-bound top, single-bound back, Sunburst or Natural finish.
- **Neck:** Bound rosewood fingerboard, double-parallelogram inlay, crown peghead inlay, pearl logo.
- **Pickups & Controls:** 1 P-90 pickup in neck position (some with 2 pickups and 3 knobs 1951–53; some with Alnico V pickup 1955, humbucker from 1957), 2 knobs.
Production; 9,964.

1950

ES-140 (¾-scale) (1950–56)
Small single-cut archtop, pointed horn
- **Body & Hardware:** 12¾-inch wide laminated maple hollowbody, *f*-holes, pointed cutaway, trapeze tailpiece, single-bound top and back.
- **Neck:** 22½-inch scale, dot inlays, Sunburst finish (Natural finish rare).
- **Pickups & Controls:** 1 P-90 pickup.
Production: 2,385.

1951

CF-100E (1951–58)
Single-cut acoustic flat-top, pointed horn
- **Body & Hardware:** 14⅛-inch wide single-cutaway flat-top, pointed horn, spruce top, mahogany back and sides.
- **Neck:** bound rosewood fingerboard, pearloid trapezoid inlays, crown peghead inlay, pearl logo (earliest with no peghead inlay and decal logo).
- **Pickups & Controls:** 1 single-coil pickup with adjustable polepieces mounted at end of fingerboard, 2 knobs.
Production: 1,257.

ES-175 double pickup (1951–53, 1971–91, 2006–current) / **ES-175D** (1953–70) / **ES-175 Reissue** (1991–2005)
Single-cut archtop, pointed horn, double-parallelogram inlay, 2 pickups
- **Body & Hardware:** 16½-inch wide, laminated maple body (mahogany back and sides 1983–90), pointed cutaway, laminated beveled-edge pickguard, rosewood bridge (Tune-o-matic from 1977), hinged tailpiece with pointed ends and 3 raised parallelograms (T-center with zigzag tubes 1958–71, hinged from 1991), triple-bound top, single-bound back, Sunburst or Natural finish.
- **Neck:** bound rosewood fingerboard, double-parallelogram inlay, crown peghead inlay, pearl logo.
- **Pickups & Controls:** 2 P-90 pickups (some with Alnico V, humbuckers from 1957), 4 knobs, toggle switch.
Production: 16,790.

L-5CES (1951–current)

Single-cut archtop, block inlay

- **Body & Hardware:** 17-inch wide, rounded cutaway (pointed cutaway 1960–69), solid carved spruce top, carved maple back (laminated 1-piece back 1960–69), maple sides, single-bound *f*-holes, multiple-bound top and back.
- **Neck:** ebony fingerboard with pointed end, block inlays, multiple-bound fingerboard and peghead, flowerpot peghead inlay.
- **Pickups & Controls:** 2 P-90 pickups (Alnico V from 1954, humbuckers from late 1957), 4 knobs, selector switch.

Production: 2,963 (1951–79).

Super 400CES (1951–current)

Single-cut archtop, large flat tailpiece, split-block inlays

- **Body & Hardware:** 18-inch wide maple body, rounded cutaway (pointed cutaway 1960–69), solid carved spruce top, carved maple back (laminated 1-piece back 1960–69), maple sides, multiple-bound top, back and *f*-holes.
- **Neck:** ebony fingerboard with pointed end, split-lock inlay, multiple-bound fingerboard and peghead, 5-piece split-diamond peghead inlay.
- **Pickups & Controls:** 2 P-90 pickups (Alnico V from 1954, humbuckers from late 1957), 4 knobs, selector switch.

Production: 1,476 (1951–79).

1952

ES-295 (1952–58, 1990–2000)

Single-cut archtop, pointed horn, gold finish

- **Body & Hardware:** 16½-inch wide laminated maple body, pointed cutaway, clear pickguard back-painted with white background and gold floral design, trapeze bridge/tailpiece combo with strings looping over bridge (Bigsby vibrola 1992–97, optional 1998), triple-bound top, single-bound back, gold-plated hardware, gold finish.

- **Neck:** bound rosewood fingerboard, 19 frets (20 from 1955), double-parallelogram inlay, crown peghead inlay.
- **Pickups & Controls:** 2 P-90 pickups with white covers (humbuckers from late 1958).

Production: 1,770 (1952–58).

Les Paul Model (1952–57)

Single-cut solidbody, carved top, trapezoid inlays, 2 humbuckers

- **Body & Hardware:** single-cutaway solidbody (SG-shape double-cutaway with pointed horns, 1961–63), carved maple top, mahogany back (1-piece mahogany 1961–63), 2-piece mahogany with maple laminate 1972–77), trapeze bridge/tailpiece combination with strings looping under bridge (wraparound 1953, Tune-o-matic from 1955, side-pull vibrato 1961–63, some with pearl-inlaid ebony tailblock 1962), bound top (unbound 1961–63) nickel-plated hardware, gold top finish (some with gold back and sides; Cherry Sunburst top from 1958–60; Cherry 1961–63, gold-top 1968–69; various finishes 1972–current).
- **Neck:** single-bound rosewood fingerboard (earliest unbound), optional fat '50s or slim '60s neck from 2002, trapezoid inlays, pearl logo, *Les Paul* signature and MODEL silkscreened on peghead (crown inlay, Les Paul on truss-rod cover, 1961–63).
- **Pickups & Controls:** 2 soapbar P-90 pickups with cream-colored cover (humbuckers 1958–63, soapbar P-90s 1968–69, humbuckers 1972–current).

Production: 9,557 (1954–60); 4,556 (1961–63, may include some SGs); 3,975 (1968–69); 10,078 (1971–79).

1953

Les Paul Custom (late 1953–63, 1968–current)

Single-cut solidbody, carved top, pearl block inlays, 5-piece diamond peghead inlay

'53

LES PAUL: THE HEN THAT LAID THE GOLDEN LOG

Having only braved the concept of a hollowbodied archtop made from laminated woods three years before, Gibson threw itself head over heels into the concept of the electric guitar in 1952 with the release of the company's first solidbody guitar, the Les Paul. At the time it was a bold move for such a traditional guitar maker.

Scorned, laughed at, jeered, chided, and derided. The concept of the solidbody electric guitar was subject to such utter disdain in some corners that it's almost hard to believe it ever came to be at all. The ridicule and mockery would have been enough to send a less self-confident inventor running for the hills. Given our more than 55 years of perspective, though, we know it just had to be; a world without the solidbody guitar? Moreover, without the Gibson Les Paul? Unthinkable.

Of course Rickenbacker had made limited numbers of solid electrics since the early 1930s, and Merle Travis and Paul A. Bigsby had together produced a few forward-looking, single-cutaway solidbodies in 1947–48, while Fender's coup in releasing the first mass-produced solidbody electric guitar in 1950 has been widely documented. Gibson, however, was one of the longest-established makers in the business, had set a standard with traditional players, and had a history and a reputation to consider. Little wonder its execs told young inventor, recording artist, and radio star Rhubarb Red to take a hike when he first started pestering them to turn his solid-cored electric into a reality in the early 1940s.

But you can't stop progress. Despite the mocking asides, that 'canoe paddle' that an upstart company from California had introduced in 1950 was starting to catch on, and slowly but surely more guitarists were stepping toward the front of the stage alongside singers, lap-steel players, and horn soloists, and they wanted to be heard. Bright, cutting, feedback-resistant – the solidbody electric was the way to do it. You can almost hear the phone call: "Uh, Mr Paul? This is Gibson. We were just wondering if you wouldn't mind popping back in for another little talk about that 'log' contraption of yours ...?"

Rather than following Fender's bolt-together, plank-bodied standards, Gibson approached the solidbody electric from the perspective of a skilled, archtop guitar-maker. It used a carved maple cap atop the solid mahogany back, and a glued-in neck that, after the first few unbound examples, would carry a bound rosewood fingerboard. The model, therefore, was already more recognizable in feel and appearance to players familiar with Gibson's hollowbody archtops, but was entirely radical all the same – reflected in its gold metallic finish.

Over the course of the decade, the Les Paul would evolve into the most desirable collector's item on the vintage market: the Sunburst 'Standard' of 1958–60. Along the way it gained an improved wrapover bridge (1953), then a Tune-o-matic bridge (1955), humbucking pickups (1957), and finally that hallowed finish in 1958. Eight years down the road it finally proved just how far ahead of its time it was by failing to rack up satisfactory sales, and Gibson radically altered the Les Paul in 1961 to make it the double-cutaway, all-mahogany-bodied guitar that would soon and forever after be known as the SG. By the mid 1960s, however, the fat, plummy, full-throated, and long-sustaining Les Paul started to show what it could really do in the hands of a number of British and American blues-rockers, and by the late 1960s and early '70s was established as the favored tool of wailing, hard-rocking lead players in particular, a position from which it has never really been toppled.

- **Body & Hardware:** single-cutaway solidbody (SG-shape double-cutaway with pointed horns, 1961–63), carved mahogany top, mahogany back (1-piece mahogany 1961–63) (4-piece "pancake" body 1969–76), Tune-o-matic bridge, stop tailpiece, optional Bigsby (listed as a separate catalog model, some with pearl-inlaid ebony tailblock 1962), multiple-bound top and back, gold-plated hardware.
- **Neck:** single-bound ebony fingerboard, pearl block inlay (*20th Anniversary* at 15th fret, 1974), *Les Paul Custom* on truss-rod cover, 5-piece split-diamond peghead inlay, pearl logo, closed-back Kluson tuners (Grover Rotomatics from 1959), plastic tulip-shaped tuner buttons.
- **Pickups & Controls:** Alnico V neck pickup (rectangular poles), black soapbar P-90 bridge pickup (most with 3 humbuckers 1957–60, 3 pickups 1961–63, 2 pickups from 1969).
Production: 1,912 (1954–60); 1,075 (1961–63, may include some SGs); 5,398 (1968–70); 50,605 (all variations 1971–79).

1954

ES-130 full-depth (1954–56), **ES-135** (1956–57)
Non-cut archtop, 1 pickup, trapezoid inlays
- **Body & Hardware:** 16¼-inch archtop body of laminated maple, trapeze tailpiece with raised diamond, laminated beveled-edge pickguard, single-bound top and back.
- **Neck:** mahogany, 24¾-inch scale, single-bound fingerboard, trapezoid inlays, decal logo, no peghead ornament, Sunburst finish.
- **Pickups & Controls:** 1 P-90 pickup mounted 1-inch from fingerboard, 2 knobs.
Production: 556.

J-160E (1954–78, 1990–96) / **J-160 Standard** (2002) / **J-160 VS Standard** (2002, 2005–current)
Dreadnought-size flat-top, pickup at end of fingerboard
- **Body & Hardware:** 16-inch wide acoustic flat-top, round-shouldered dreadnought shape (square-shouldered 1969–78), spruce top, mahogany back and sides, 2 large saddle-height adjustment screws nuts (small nuts from 1959).
- **Neck:** bound rosewood fingerboard, trapezoid inlays, crown peghead inlay, pearl logo.
- **Pickups & Controls:** 1 single-coil pickup with adjustable polepieces mounted at end of fingerboard, 2 knobs.
Production: 6,988 (1954–79).

Les Paul Junior (1954–63, 1986–92) (2001–02)
Single-cut solidbody, 1 P-90 pickup, Les Paul Junior *on headstock*
- **Body & Hardware:** solid mahogany body with flat top (double-cutaway with rounded horns 1958–60, thinner SG-style with pointed horns 1961–63, single-cutaway 1986–92), stud-mounted bridge / tailpiece, tortoiseshell plastic pickguard (black laminated from 1961), Maestro vibrato optional from 1962, nickel-plated hardware (chrome 1986–92).
- **Neck:** unbound rosewood fingerboard, 16 frets clear of body (22 frets clear from 1958), dot inlays, plastic tuner buttons (metal (1986–92), yellow silkscreen logo and model name on peghead, decal logo.
- **Pickups & Controls:** 1 black P-90 pickup with "dog-ear" cover (stacked-coil P-100 1990–92), 2 knobs.
Production: 19,035 (1954–60), 6,864 (1961–63, may include some SGs).

Les Paul TV (1954–59)
Single- or double-cut solidbody, Limed Mahogany finish, 1 P-90
- **Body & Hardware:** solid mahogany body with flat top (double-cutaway with rounded horns from 1958), stud-mounted bridge/tailpiece, tortoiseshell plastic pickguard, nickel-plated hardware, Limed Mahogany finish (early with Natural finish).
- **Neck:** unbound rosewood fingerboard, yellow silkscreen logo and model name on peghead, decal logo.

- **Pickups & Controls:** 1 black P-90 pickup with "dog-ear" cover.

Production: 2,270.

Super 300CES (1954)
Single-cut archtop, 18-inch wide, double-parallelogram inlays

- **Body & Hardware:** 18-inch wide maple body, carved spruce top, triple-bound top and back, tailpiece with 3 cutouts, laminated beveled-edge pickguard.
- **Neck:** single-bound fingerboard with square end, double-parallelogram inlay, single-bound headstock, crown headstock inlay.
- **Pickups & Controls:** 1 or 2 P-90 pickup.

L-5 CEST (1954–62, 1983): thinline body, rounded cutaway, 2 humbuckers (1 floating humbucker in 1983).

1955

Byrdland (1955–current)
Thinbody archtop, short-scale version of L-5CES, pearl block inlays. Billy Byrd/Hank Garland model

- **Body & Hardware:** 17-inch wide, rounded cutaway (a few double-cutaway, 1958–62, pointed cutaway 1960–69), 2¼-inch deep, carved spruce top, carved maple back, triple-loop tubular tailpiece, tortoiseshell celluloid pickguard (a few early with pearloid), 7-ply top binding, triple-bound back, 7-ply pickguard binding, single-bound *f*-holes, gold-plated hardware, Sunburst or Natural finish.
- **Neck:** ebony fingerboard with pointed end, 5-ply fingerboard binding, 23½-inch scale, pearl block inlays, flowerpot peghead inlay, 7-ply peghead binding.
- **Pickups & Controls:** 2 Alnico V pickups (humbuckers from late 1957, a few with 1 humbucker and 1 Charlie Christian).

Production: 2,670 (1955–79).

ES-5 Switchmaster (1955–62)
Single-cut archtop, 3 pickups, 6 knobs

- **Body & Hardware:** 17-inch wide, rounded cutaway (pointed 1960–62), Tune-o-matic bridge 1955, trapeze tailpiece (tubular with double loop from 1956), laminated beveled-edge pickguard, 5-ply binding, gold-plated hardware, Sunburst or Natural finish.
- **Neck:** 2-piece maple neck with stripe down center, pointed-end rosewood fingerboard with 5-ply binding, large pearl block inlays, single-bound peghead, black "stinger" on back of peghead, crown peghead inlay.
- **Pickups & Controls:** 3 P-90 pickups (humbuckers from 1957), 6 knobs (3 volume, 3 tone), slotted pickup selector switch on cutaway bout.

Production: 498 (1956–71).

ES-350T (1955–63, 1977–80, 1992–93, 1998–99)
Thinbody single-cut archtop, rounded horn, double-parallelogram inlays

- **Body & Hardware:** 17-inch wide body of laminated maple, rounded cutaway (pointed cutaway 1960–63), Tune-o-matic bridge, tailpiece with W-shape tubular design, laminated beveled-edge pickguard, triple-bound top and back, Sunburst or Natural finish, gold-plated hardware.
- **Neck:** 23¾-inch scale (25½-inch from 1977), single-bound fingerboard and peghead, double-parallelogram inlay, crown peghead inlay.
- **Pickups & Controls:** 2 P-90 pickups (humbuckers from mid 1957).

Production: 1,041 (1955–63); 481 (1977–79).

Les Paul Special (1955–59) (1989–97)
Single- or double-cut solidbody, flat top, 2 P-90s

- **Body & Hardware:** single cutaway mahogany solidbody (double cutaway with rounded horns 1959, single cutaway 1989–97), flat top, nickel-plated hardware, Limed Mahogany finish (a few very early with Natural finish).
- **Neck:** bound rosewood fingerboard, dot inlays,

AN INTONATION REVELATION: THE TUNE-O-MATIC BRIDGE

Prior to the arrival of the Tune-o-matic bridge in 1954, Gibson electrics carried either a floating bridge with compensated one-piece rosewood or ebony saddle, a rudimentary trapeze tailpiece with integral bridge bar, or a stud-mounted wraparound bridge, each of which offered only the crudest global intonation and height-adjustment facilities. When the Tune-o-matic bridge, also known as the ABR-1, first appeared – initially on the black Les Paul Custom and then on the goldtop Les Paul 'Standard' the following year – it was a true revelation in intonation, and set a standard for simplicity and functionality for bridges of its ilk.

The Tune-o-matic was designed by Gibson president Ted McCarty himself, and on solidbody guitars was partnered with a separate 'stud' or 'stop-bar' tailpiece, which was essentially a modified version of the wraparound bridge. The pair provided both a firm seating for the strings at the body-end termination point of their speaking length, and a facility for adjusting the individual length of each via a sliding steel saddle and adjustment screw. Finally a player could fine-tune intonation for themselves, in a matter of minutes, and easily adjust it again when atmospheric conditions required periodic alterations. This solid, well-anchored piece of hardware also yields good coupling between string and body, which results in solid tone and excellent sustain. Gibson has also employed the Tune-o-matic bridge on a number of archtop electrics over the years, where it is partnered either with a trapeze tailpiece on hollowbody models such as the ES-175, or a stop-bar tailpiece on semi-acoustic models with solid center blocks, such as the ES-335.

pearl peghead logo, yellow silkscreen model name, pearl logo.
- **Pickups & Controls:** 2 black soapbar P-90 pickups (P-100 stacked-coil humbuckers 1989–97), 4 knobs, toggle switch on upper bass bout.
Production: 5,949 (1954–59, also see SG Special 1959–60).

1956

ES-125T (1956–68): Thinline body.
Production: 9,640.
See earlier listing for ES-125

ES-225T (1956–58)
Thinbody single-cut archtop, pointed horn, dot inlay
- **Body & Hardware:** 16¼-inch wide, pointed cutaway, trapeze bridge/tailpiece combination with strings looping over bridge, laminated beveled-edge pickguard, single-bound top and back, Sunburst or Natural finish.
- **Neck:** bound rosewood fingerboard, dot inlays, pearl logo, no peghead ornament.
- **Pickups & Controls:** P-90 pickup in middle position, 2 knobs.
Production: 5,220.

ES-225TD (1956–59): 2 pickups.
Production: 2,754.

Les Paul Junior ¾-scale (1956–61): Shorter neck, 22¾-inch scale, 14 frets clear of body (15 clear from 1959)
Production: 787.

1957

ES-125T (¾-scale) (1957–68): Thinline body 12½-inch wide, 22½-inch scale.
Production: 1,582.

'58

BUCKING THE HUM

At the urging of company president Ted McCarty, Gibson technicians Seth Lover and Walt Fuller began working on the idea of a hum-rejecting guitar pickup in 1955. Lover, a radio and electronics expert, had worked for Gibson on and off in the 1940s, and, after rejoining the company in 1952, had developed the single-coil Alnico pickup, as used briefly – but most famously – in the neck position of the Les Paul Custom, as well as on a few archtop models. Gibson's main pickup of the day, the P-90, had a full, fat, distinctive tone, but, like all single-coil pickups, was prone to picking up unwanted hum and noise from external electrical sources. Being familiar with tube amplifiers, Lover was well aware of how a 'choke' (a coil or small transformer) could help filter out hum induced by an amp's power supply, and began working toward applying the same logic to guitar pickups. His solution took the form of a double-coil pickup, in which the two coils were placed side by side, wired together out of phase with each other, and given opposite magnetic polarities. As a result, this configuration rejected much of the hum that single-coil pickups reproduce – which is eliminated when two like but reverse-phase signals are summed together – but passed along all of the guitar tone. Lover also added a thin nickel cover to the pickups, to further reject electrostatic interference. In addition to the benefits regarding noise rejection, the double-coil pickup's side-by-side coil alignment produced a bigger and rounder sound than that of the average single-coil pickup.

Gibson dubbed Lover's new creation the 'humbucker' for its ability to 'buck' electrical hum and, aware that it was a unique device in the fledgling industry, applied for a US patent to protect the design. The first humbucker used by Gibson in production was a triple-coil version that appeared on lap steel guitars in 1956. When the now-familiar double-coil humbuckers arrived in 1957 on the goldtop and Custom Les Paul models, and on archtop electrics such as the ES-175, they carried stickers that read "Patent Applied For", to ward off would-be copyists while the company awaited the patent. Pickups of the era, therefore, are given the nickname 'PAF', which applies to any pickup carrying the "Patent Applied For" sticker all Gibson humbuckers wore between 1957 and late 1962.

The first 'patent number pickups', as the post-PAF humbuckers have come to be known, were almost identical to the final stocks of PAFs, which had become fairly consistent in their construction by 1962. But earlier examples of the late 1950s had varied quite widely and, as any collector knows, there are 'great, greater and greatest' versions out there (if you will). Gibson used a range of Alnico magnet types in constructing these pickups – from Alnico II through Alnico V, largely determined by whatever stocks the company could lay its hands on in the day – and, because coil winding was a hand-guided process, pickup coils were wound to different numbers of turns, too, and therefore differing strengths. In addition to these constructional variables, another purely cosmetic variable has sent many collectors in search of the rare and ultra-rare examples: when Gibson ran short of black plastic coil formers, or 'bobbins', it bought in cream stock, so double-cream and black-and-cream PAFs – dubbed 'zebra stripes' – can also be found beneath some pickups' metal covers.

PAFs are not really much hotter, in electrical terms, than the average P-90, and the two different pickup types from the same era generally show similar DC resistance readings in the 7.5k to 8.5k ohms range. But the humbucker's broader sonic window sends a meatier spread of frequencies to the amp, which creates a fatter, warmer sound, and can also drive an amp more easily into distortion if needed. However, a good PAF still has good treble response and excellent definition.

ES-125TD (1957–63): 2 pickups.
Production: 1,215.

ES-140T (¾-scale T) (1957–67): Thin body.
Production: 1,533.

1958

EDS-1275 Double 12 (1958–68, 1974–current)
6-string neck and 12-string neck
- **Body & Hardware:** hollow body with maple back
  and sides and carved spruce top, double cutaway
  with pointed horns, (SG-style solidbody with
  pointed horns from c1962), no soundholes, Tune-
  o-matic bridges, triple-bound top and back
  (unbound with change to SG shape), nickel-plated
  hardware (gold on Alpine White finish from 1988).
- **Neck:** 12-string and 6-string necks, 24¾-inch
  scales, bound rosewood fingerboards, double-
  parallelogram inlay, pearl logo (decal from 1977).
- **Pickups & Controls:** 2 humbucking pickups for
  each neck, 2 knobs for each neck, 1 switch on
  treble side, 1 switch on bass side, 1 switch
  between bridges (with change to SG body:
  4 knobs on lower treble bout, 1 switch between
  tailpieces, 1 switch on upper treble bout).
Production: 110 (1958–68); 1,145 (1974–79).

EMS-1235 Double Mandolin (1958–68)
*Short 6-string guitar neck and standard 6-string
guitar neck*
- **Body & Hardware:** double pointed cutaways,
  hollow maple body with carved spruce top, no
  soundholes (SG-style solidbody with pointed
  cutaways from c1962), Tune-o-matic bridge for
  standard neck, height-adjustable bridge for short
  neck.
- **Neck:** standard guitar neck and short 6-string
  neck with 15½-inch scale, bound rosewood
  fingerboards, double-parallelogram inlay, no
  peghead ornament.
- **Pickups & Controls:** 1 humbucking pickup for

short neck, 2 humbucking pickups for standard
neck, 4 knobs on lower treble bout, 1 switch
between tailpieces, 1 switch on upper treble bout.
Production: 61.

ES-335TD (1958–81) / **ES-335 DOT** (1981–90) /
ES-335 Reissue (1991–98) / **ES-335 Dot**
(1999–current)
*Thinbody double-cutaway archtop, 2 humbuckers,
dot or small block inlays*
- **Body & Hardware:** 16-inch semi-hollowbody of
  laminated maple, 1⅝-inch deep, double-cutaway,
  rounded horns, Tune-o-matic bridge, stop
  tailpiece (trapeze from 1964), Bigsby vibrato
  optional (most models with Bigsby have CUSTOM
  MADE plate covering original tailpiece holes; some
  without holes or plate), laminated beveled-edge
  pickguard extends below bridge (shorter guard
  from 1961, longer guard from), single-bound top
  and back, plain or figured top optional from 2006,
  satin or gloss finish optional from 2006.
- **Neck:** single-bound rosewood fingerboard, neck-
  body joint at 19th fret, dot inlay (small pearloid
  blocks from 1962; some with single-parallelogram
  1960s), crown peghead inlay (early with unbound
  fingerboard and no peghead ornament).
- **Pickups & Controls:** 2 humbucking pickups,
  2 tone and 2 volume knobs, 1 switch, coil tap
  switch 1977–81.
Production: 23,571 (1958–70); 26,781 (1971–79).

ES-355TD (1958–71, 1994, 1997, 2004)
*Thinbody double-cut archtop, 2 humbuckers, block
inlays*
- **Body & Hardware:** 16-inch semi-hollowbody of
  laminated maple, 1⅝-inch deep, double-cutaway,
  rounded horns, Tune-o-matic bridge, Bigsby
  vibrato (SW sideways-action vibrato optional, lyre
  vibrato 1963–68), multiple-bound pickguard
  extends below bridge, multiple-bound top, triple-
  bound back, single-bound f-holes.
- **Neck:** single-bound ebony fingerboard, large
  block inlays, multiple-bound peghead, 5-piece

split-diamond peghead inlay, Grover Rotomatic tuners.

- **Pickups & Controls:** 2 humbucking pickups, mono circuitry standard but stereo with Varitone more common

Production: 3,151 (1958–70); 2,029 (1971–79).

Explorer (1958–59, 1975–79) / **Explorer I** (1981–82) / **Explorer 83** (1983) / **Explorer** (1984–89) / **Explorer Reissue** (1990) / **Explorer '76** (1991–2003) / **X-Plorer** (2003–current)

Angular solidbody, six-on-a-side tuners

- **Body & Hardware:** Korina (African limba wood) body (mahogany from 1975, some Korina 1976, alder 1982–84, mahogany from 1986), elongated upper treble bout and lower bass bout, Tune-o-matic bridge, stop tailpiece, optional vibrato 1981–89, white pickguard (no pickguard 1984–89).
- **Neck:** unbound rosewood fingerboard (ebony optional 1983–86, ebony 1987–88, rosewood 1989, ebony or rosewood from 1990), dot inlays, scimitar-shape peghead curves to treble side (a few early with forked peghead), pearl logo (decal 1981–89).
- **Pickups & Controls:** 2 humbucking pickups, 3 knobs in straight line, selector switch on treble horn (knobs in triangular configuration, switch near knobs 1984–89, in straight line from 1990).

Production: 19 (1958); 3 (1959); 175 (1966–70).

Flying V (1958–59, 1965–69, 1971–79, 1984–89 / **Flying V I** (1981–82) / **Flying V 83** (1983) / **Flying V Reissue** (1990) / **Flying V '67** (1991–2003) / **X-Factor V** (2003–current)

V-shaped solidbody

- **Body & Hardware:** Korina (African limba wood) V-shaped solidbody (mahogany 1965–79, alder 1981–89, mahogany from 1990), some *Limited Edition Reissue* medallion on top 1971–74, strings anchor through body in V-shaped anchor plate (stopbar or vibrato from 1965), white pickguard (a few early with black, no pickguard 1981–89),

body shoulders square at neck, gold-plated hardware (chrome from 1965).

- **Neck:** unbound rosewood fingerboard (ebony 1981–83, rosewood or ebony 1981–88), dot inlays, triangular peghead with rounded top, raised plastic peghead logo (logo on truss-rod cover from 1965–79, decal from 1981).
- **Pickups & Controls:** 2 humbucking pickups (exposed-coil 1975–79), 3 knobs in straight line (triangular knob configuration from 1965.

Production: 81 (1958); 17 (1959); 2 (1965); 111 (1966); 15 (1969); 47 (1970); 350 (1971); 2 (1973); 1 (1974), 3,223 (1975–79).

L-4CES (1958, 1969, 1986–2003) / **L-4CES Mahogany** (2004–06)

Single-cut archtop, pointed horn, spruce top

- **Body & Hardware:** 16½-inch archtop, solid spruce top, maple back and sides (mahogany from 1986, solid carved mahogany back from 2004), triple-bound top, single-bound back (triple-bound from 1986).
- **Neck:** bound rosewood fingerboard, double-parallelogram inlay, crown peghead inlay.
- **Pickups & Controls:** Charlie Christian pickup (2 humbuckers from 1986), 2 knobs (4 knobs on lower treble bout, switch on upper bass bout from 1986).

Production: 9 (1969).

1959

ES-330T (1959–63)

Thinbody double-cut archtop, P-90 pickup

- **Body & Hardware:** 16-inch hollow thinbody archtop of laminated maple, double rounded cutaways, Tune-o-matic bridge, trapeze tailpiece, single-bound top and back, Sunburst or Natural finish.
- **Neck:** joins body at 17th fret, bound rosewood fingerboard, dot inlay (small blocks from 1962), pearl logo, no peghead ornament.
- **Pickups & Controls:** 1 black plastic-covered

RADICAL ANGLES AND A SEMI-HOLLOW STANDARD

The year 1958 was one of significant advancement for Gibson, although the fruits of some of the company's forward thinking of the time would take many years to fully ripen. We have already seen that this is the year the Les Paul evolved into the Sunburst model with humbucking pickups, but 1958 also marked the release of three entirely new designs: the ES-335 and, in the Modernistic Series, the Flying V and Explorer. The latter two, with their sharp, angular lines and space-aged styling, were so radical that they could hardly have expected to fare well in an industry that had had trouble accepting at all the concept of a solidbody guitar earlier that same decade, but Gibson was making a bid for dominance of the newly emergent rock'n'roll market and was apparently willing to take a daring step into the future. The move failed on just about all counts but, like the Les Paul, the Flying V and Explorer would both become rock icons later in the 1960s when both the style and the sound of the music had caught up to what these guitars had to offer. Fewer than 200 units of both models were made before they were withdrawn in 1960, with a few dozen more made up from leftover parts later in the '60s.

With the ES-335, on the other hand, Gibson hit the nail on the head right from the start. Thanks to its arched top and ƒ-holes, the ES-335 bore recognizable links to its lineage, but a quick probe inside its double-cutaway, thinline body, with solid center block, revealed it as a brave new design. More subtle in its advancement of the template, it was in many ways no less revolutionary, and also more acceptable to players who were hesitant to strut too far ahead of the pack. The new ES-335 had the advantage of possessing some of the familiar ES features, and in particular was only a few steps away from thinline hollowbody models such as the Byrdland and ES-350T of 1955, or the laminated ES-175 introduced in 1949, but that chunk of maple that ran down its middle to render it a semi-acoustic made a world of difference to its performance. The solid wood meant the ES-335 could carry a Tune-o-matic bridge and stopbar tailpiece, all of which worked together to produce a quick response, great note definition and the kind of sustain that couldn't be had from any fully hollow archtop on the market, thinline or full-bodied. To top it all off, plugging up the center of the body achieved impressive resistance to feedback, a major pest to archtop players of the day. Taken up quickly by adventurous jazz, country, and rock'n'roll players who recognized its advantages, the ES-335 rapidly proved itself equally at home in the hands of blues, pop, and rock players too. One of the most versatile electric guitars ever produced, it has been a Gibson mainstay ever since.

P-90 pickup in middle position (chrome cover from 1962).
Production: 2,510.

ES-330TD (1959–71) (1998–99): 2 black plastic-covered P-90 pickups, neck joins at 20th fret from 1968.
Production: 21,379 (1959–75).

ES-345TD (1959–82) (2002) / **ES-345 Reissue**

(2003–current)
Thinbody double-cut archtop, 2 humbuckers, double-parallelogram inlays
• **Body & Hardware:** 16-inch semi-hollow body of laminated maple, 1⅝-inch deep, double rounded cutaways, Tune-o-matic bridge, stop tailpiece (trapeze from 1964, stopbar from 1982), laminated beveled-edge pickguard extends below bridge (shorter guard from 1961), single-bound top and back, gold-plated hardware.

- **Neck:** single-bound rosewood fingerboard, neck-body joint at 19th fret, double-parallelogram inlay, crown peghead inlay (early with unbound fingerboard and no peghead ornament).
- **Pickups & Controls:** 2 humbucking pickups, 2 tone and 2 volume knobs, 1 selector switch, stereo electronics with two jacks, Vari-tone rotary tone selector, black ring around Vari-tone switch (gold ring from 1960).

Production: 7,240 (1958–70); 4,348 (1971–79).

Melody Maker/MM (1959–70, 1986–92) (also see Les Paul Melody Maker)

Thin single- or double-cut solidbody, oblong pickup

- **Body & Hardware:** single rounded cutaway (symmetrical double cutaway with rounded horns, 1961–62; horns slightly more open, 1963–64; SG shape with pointed horns, 1965–70; single cutaway 1986–92, body 1⅜-inch deep, wraparound bridge/tailpiece, pickguard surrounds pickups, vibrato optional from 1962.
- **Neck:** unbound rosewood fingerboard, dot inlays, narrow (2¼-inch) peghead (standard width 1970, narrow 1986–92), decal logo.
- **Pickups & Controls:** ⅞-inch-wide oblong pickup (⅝-inch from 1960) with black plastic cover and no visible poles, 2 knobs.

Production: 23,006 (1959–70)

MM ¾-scale (1959–70): 22¾-inch scale, 12 frets clear of body.

Production: 3,356.

SG Special (1959–70, 1972–78, 1985–current) / **Gibson Special** (1985), also see Special I, Special II

Double-cut solidbody, pointed horns, dots or small block inlays, 2 pickups

- **Body & Hardware:** solid mahogany double-cutaway body, rounded horns (SG-style pointed horns from 1961), pickguard does not surround pickups (larger pickguard surrounds pickups 1966–70, no pickguard 1986–90, larger pickguard from 1991), wraparound bridge (Maestro vibrato optional 1962–64, vibrato standard 1965–70, rectangular-base Tune-o-matic 1972, regular Tune-o-matic from 1973, Kahler Flyer vibrato optional 1985, Floyd Rose vibrato optional 1986).
- **Neck:** bound rosewood fingerboard (unbound from 1985, ebony from 1986, rosewood from 1996), dot inlay (small blocks 1973–85, dots from 1986), SG on truss-rod cover from 1996, pearl logo (decal from 1985).
- **Pickups & Controls:** 2 black soapbar P-90 pickups (black-covered mini-humbuckers 1972–78, 1 or 2 exposed-coil humbuckers 1985, 2 humbuckers from 1986), 4 knobs (3 knobs 1985–95, 4 from 1996), 1 switch.

Production: 22,295 (1960–70), 9,363 (1971–79).

SG Special ¾-scale (1959–61): 22-inch scale, no model name on peghead, Cherry finish.

1960

ES-125TCD (1960): 2 P-90 pickups.
Production: 287.

MM-D/Melody Maker Double 1st version
(1960–70, 1976): 2 pickups, 4 knobs standard peghead size.
Production: 19,456 (1960–70).

SG TV (1960–67)

Double-cut solidbody, pointed horns, yellow finish, 1 P-90 pickup

- **Neck:** solid mahogany double-cutaway body, pointed horns, Maestro vibrato optional (standard 1965–70), TV Yellow finish.
- **Neck:** unbound rosewood fingerboard, dot inlay.
- **Pickups & Controls:** 1 "dog ear" P-90 pickup (soapbar 1966–67).

Production: 3,480.

1961

Barney Kessel Custom (1961–73)

Double-cut archtop, pointed horns, bowtie inlay

- **Body & Hardware:** 17-inch wide, full-depth body, laminated spruce top (some with laminated maple 1961–64, standard from 1965), double pointed cutaways, gold-plated hardware, Cherry Sunburst finish.
- **Neck:** maple, bound rosewood fingerboard, 25½-inch scale, bowtie inlay, bound peghead, musical note peghead inlay.
- **Pickups & Controls:** 2 humbucking pickups, Tune-o-matic bridge, trapeze tailpiece with raised diamond, model name on wood tailpiece insert, laminated beveled-edge pickguard, triple-bound top and back.

Production: 740.

Barney Kessel Regular (1961–73): Mahogany neck, double-parallelogram inlay, crown peghead inlay, nickel-plated hardware. Production: 1,117.

Crest Special (1961–63, 1969)

Thinbody single-cut archtop, crest on peghead

- **Body & Hardware:** thinhollowbody, carved spruce top, pointed cutaway, crest-shaped insert in trapeze tailpiece, gold-plated hardware, some labeled *L-5CT Spec.*
- **Neck:** ebony fingerboard, slashed-block (Super 400 style) inlay, crest peghead inlay with 3 crescent moons and castle.
- **Pickups & Controls:** 2 humbucking pickups, Varitone control.

ES-125TC (1961–69): Thinline body, pointed cutaway. Production: 5,234.

ES-125TDC (1961–70): 2 P-90 pickups: Production: 5,556.

Johnny Smith (1961–88) / **Chet Atkins (JS) Double**

(1989–91) / **Le Grand** (1993–current)

Single-cut archtop, floating pickup, split-block inlays

- **Body & Hardware:** 17-inch wide, 3⅜-inch deep (not as deep as L-5), single rounded cutaway, X-braced carved spruce top, maple back and sides, adjustable ebony bridge, L-5 style tailpiece with model name on center insert (TP-6 6-finger from 1979), multiple-bound top and back, gold-plated hardware, Sunburst or Natural finish.
- **Neck:** 25-inch scale, multiple-bound ebony fingerboard with square end, split-block inlays, multiple-bound peghead, 5-piece split-diamond peghead inlay.
- 1 floating mini-humbucking pickup (some with experimental pickups 1989–91), knobs on pickguard.

Production: 963 (1962–79).

1962

EBSF-1250 (1962–68)

Bass neck and 6-string neck

- **Body & Hardware:** SG-style solid mahogany body pointed horns, beveled edges.
- **Neck:** 4-string bass neck and 6-string guitar neck, rosewood fingerboards, double-parallelogram inlays.
- **Pickups & Controls:** 2 humbucking pickups for each neck, 4 knobs on lower treble bout, 1 switch between tailpieces, 1 switch on upper treble bout, fuzz-tone on bass.

Production: 22.

ES-120T (1962–70)

Thinbody archtop, pickup and controls in molded pickguard

- **Body & Hardware:** 16½-inch wide thinline body, 1 *f*-hole, single-bound top and back, Sunburst finish.
- **Neck:** unbound rosewood fingerboard, dot inlays, decal logo.
- **Pickups & Controls:** Melody Maker pickup,

knobs and jack all mounted in large molded pickguard.
Production: 8,895.

Tal Farlow Signature (1962–67, 1993–current)
Single-cut archtop, simulated scroll in cutaway bout
- **Body & Hardware:** full-depth archtop of laminated maple, deep rounded cutaway, binding material inlaid in cutaway to simulate scroll, 4-point single-bound pickguard, Tune-o-matic bridge, trapeze tailpiece with raised diamond, model name on wood tailpiece insert, triple-bound top, Viceroy Brown finish (Wine Red added 1993).
- **Neck:** 25½-inch scale, bound fingerboard, fingerboard inlay like inverted J-200 crest inlay, bound peghead, double-crown peghead inlay.
- **Pickups & Controls:** 2 humbucking pickups, toggle switch just below pickguard.
Production: 215 (1962–67).

1963

Firebird I, reverse-body (1963–65, 1991–92) / **1963 Firebird I** (2000–current)
Solidbody with treble horn larger than bass horn, 1 mini-humbucker
- **Body & Hardware:** angular body, 9-piece mahogany/walnut neck-through-body with mahogany side wings, 3-ply white-black-white pickguard with beveled edge, wraparound bridge with raised integral saddles, no vibrato, (a few with Firebird III vibrato), nickel-plated hardware (gold-plated, 1991–92).
- **Neck:** unbound rosewood fingerboard, dot inlays, 6 tuners all on treble side of peghead, beveled peghead edge, Kluson banjo-style tuners, logo on truss-rod cover.
- **Pickups & Controls:** 1 mini-humbucking pickup with no polepieces, 2 knobs.
Production: 1,377 (1963–65, includes some non-reverse).

Firebird III, reverse-body (1963–65) / **1964 Firebird III** (2000–current)
Solidbody with treble horn larger than bass horn, 2 mini-humbuckers, dot inlays
- **Body & Hardware:** treble horn larger than bass horn, 9-piece mahogany/walnut neck-through-body with mahogany side wings, 3-ply white-black-white pickguard with beveled edge, wraparound bridge with raised integral saddles, simple spring vibrato with flat arm.
- **Neck:** single-bound rosewood fingerboard, dot inlays, tuners all on treble side of peghead (all on bass side, 1965), Kluson banjo-style tuners (some with right-angle tuners, 1965), logo on truss-rod cover.
- **Pickups & Controls:** 2 mini-humbucking pickups with no polepieces, 3-way toggle switch.
Production: 2,546 (1963–65, includes some non-reverse).

Firebird V, reverse-body (1963–65, 1986–87) / **Firebird Reissue** (1990) / **Firebird V** (1991–current) / **1964 Firebird V** (Custom Shop, 2000–current)
Solidbody with treble horn larger than bass horn, 2 mini-humbuckers, trapezoid inlays
- **Body & Hardware:** treble horn larger than bass horn, 9-piece mahogany/walnut neck-through-body(7-piece from 1990) with mahogany side wings (all mahogany body with solid finish colors from 2002), 3-ply white-black-white pickguard with beveled edge, Tune-o-matic bridge, Deluxe vibrato with metal tailpiece cover engraved with Gibson and leaf-and-lyre (Kahler vibrato or stopbar tailpiece optional, 1986–87; no vibrola from 1990).
- **Neck:** single-bound rosewood fingerboard, trapezoid inlays, tuners all on treble side of peghead (all on bass side, 1965, 1991–current), Kluson banjo-style tuners (some with right-angle tuners, 1965), logo on truss-rod cover.
- **Pickups & Controls:** 2 mini-humbucking pickups with no polepieces, 3-way toggle switch.
Production: 925 (1963–65, includes some non-reverse).

Firebird VII, reverse-body (1963–65, 1991–93, 2003–current) / **1965 Firebird VII** (Custom Shop 2000–current)

Solidbody with treble horn larger than bass horn, 3 mini-humbuckers, block inlays

- **Body & Hardware:** treble horn larger than bass horn, 9-piece mahogany/walnut neck-through-body with mahogany side wings (all-mahogany body with red metallic finish, 2002–current), 3-ply white-black-white pickguard with beveled edge, Tune-o-matic bridge, Deluxe vibrato (tubular lever arm with plastic end cap, metal tailpiece cover engraved with Gibson and leaf-and-lyre decoration), gold-plated hardware (chrome-plated 1991–93).
- **Neck:** single-bound ebony fingerboard, block inlay beginning at 1st fret, tuners all on treble side of peghead (all on bass side, 1965), beveled peghead edge, large Kluson banjo-style tuners, logo on truss-rod cover.
- **Pickups & Controls:** 3 mini-humbucking pickups with no polepieces, 3-way toggle switch, pearl block inlay (aged inlay 1991–93).

Production: 303 (1963–65, includes some non-reverse).

Johnny Smith Double (1963–89): 2 floating mini-humbucking pickups. Production: 625 (1962–79).

SG Custom (1963–79) / **SG '62 Custom** (1986) / **SG Les Paul Custom** (1987–90) / **Les Paul/SG Custom Reissue** (1997–2005) / **SG Custom** (2006–current)

Double-cut solidbody, pointed horns, pearl block inlays.

- **Body & Hardware:** double-cutaway mahogany solidbody with pointed horns, vibrato with lyre and logo on coverplate (Bigsby optional 1972–79, stopbar 1986–2001, Maestro optional from 2002), small pickguard does not surround pickups (larger pickguard 1966–71, wing-shaped 1972, small pickguard from 1972), Vintage Original Spec aging treatment optional from 2006.

- **Neck:** ebony fingerboard, pearl block inlays, 5-piece split-diamond peghead inlay.
- **Pickups & Controls:** 3 humbucking pickups, 4 knobs, 1 switch (controls on semi-circular plate 1972).

Production: 1,566 (1964–70, also see Les Paul Custom 1961–63); 3,705 (1971–79).

SG Junior (1963–70, 1991–93)

Double-cut solidbody, pointed horns, 1 P-90. Also see Les Paul Junior 1961–63.

- **Body & Hardware:** double-cutaway solid mahogany body, pointed horns, Maestro vibrato optional (standard 1965–70), Cherry finish.
- **Neck:** unbound rosewood fingerboard, dot inlays, decal logo.
- **Pickups & Controls:** 1 "dog ear" P-90 pickup (soapbar 1966–70), 2 knobs.

Production: 12,133 (1964–70, also see Les Paul Junior 1961–63).

SG Standard (1963–70 1972–80 1983–86 1988–current) (also see SG Reissue, The SG)

Double-cut solidbody, pointed horns, trapezoid inlays.

- **Body & Hardware:** double-cutaway solid mahogany body, pointed horns (walnut 1981), pickguard does not surround pickups (larger pickguard surrounds pickups 1966–86, small pickguard 1988–90, large pickguard from 1991), Tune-o-matic bridge (rectangular bridge base (1972–73), Maestro vibrato (up-and-down pull) with lyre and logo on coverplate (no vibrato 1972–75, Bigsby optional 1976–80).
- **Neck:** mahogany (walnut 1981), bound rosewood fingerboard (unbound 1972–81), trapezoid inlay (small blocks 1972–80, dots 1981, small blocks 1983–86, trapezoids from 1988), crown peghead inlay, pearl logo, no *Les Paul* on truss-rod cover.
- **Pickups & Controls:** 2 humbucking pickups with metal covers (black plastic covers 1973–80, no covers 1981), 4 knobs, selector switch by

'63

'64

SOARING BACKWARDS, AND FORWARDS: THE FIREBIRD

Not as rare as the Flying V and Explorer, nor as highly prized as the 1958–60 Les Paul, the 'reverse-bodied' Firebirds of the early 1960s are nevertheless very high up on the desirability ladder for vintage Gibson guitars. The model illustrates another of Gibson's efforts to out-rock'n'roll the likes of Fender and Gretsch, and carries the kinds of curves and colorful finishes that indicate a keen rivalry with Leo's creations in particular. Many makers of the day were looking to the chrome-and-tailfins panache of Detroit in the golden era of the auto industry for their esthetic inspiration. Gibson went right to the source for the look of its new model by hiring car designer Ray Dietrich. The result was an instrument that, once again, conveyed a musical style that was a few years ahead of its time. The lower bout had something of the offset flare of the Explorer, although with more rounded corners, while the recessed bass-side upper bout and elongated treble-side horn slightly invoked a flipped-over Fender Jazzmaster, hence the 'reverse-bodied' nickname that the model took on between its arrival in 1963 and the redesign in 1965. In addition, the Firebird had a reversed six-a-side headstock shaped like a stylized falcon head, with 'banjo' tuners that had their buttons extending toward the back of the headstock so as not to spoil the look.

Also arguably lifted from Fender, although again originally inspired by the car industry, was the custom color palette that Gibson made available to the Firebird range. To dress up the model, which came standard in Tobacco Sunburst, customers could order their Firebird (or any Gibson, technically) in Ember Red, Cardinal Red, Polaris White, Golden Mist, Silver Mist, Heather, Pelham Blue, Frost Blue, Kerry Green, or Inverness Green. Beyond the colors and the body and headstock lines, the Firebird was constructed differently from any Gibson that had gone before. Its solid mahogany body was made from two 'wings' glued to a slightly raised center block that extended the length of the neck – what has become known as a 'through neck' – and its pickups were a variation of the bright, cutting mini humbuckers that Gibson had inherited from Epiphone, although without the protruding adjustment screws. The Firebird I had a single pickup at the bridge, dot position markers and a wraparound bridge; the III had two pickups, dots, and a Maestro vibrola; the V had two pickups, Maestro, and trapezoid inlays; and the VII had three pickups, Maestro, block inlays and gold-plated hardware.

A few years after its arrival the Firebird would find its way into the hands of Brian Jones of the Rolling Stones, Phil Manzanera of Roxy Music, bluesman Johnny Winter, and others, but it failed to set the world of rock'n'roll alight in its day, and sales were meager. Gibson redesigned the model in 1965 – an update also driven in part by Fender's objection to the 'reverse-bodied' versions' similarity to the offset-waist body of the Jazzmaster and Jaguar, which Fender had patented. The result was a less dramatic, though still fairly distinctive guitar. Funny enough, the 'right way around' body of the new 'non-reverse' Firebirds, as they have come to be known, got all the horns and bulges closer to the positions they held on the Fender guitars, but they were now slightly 'melted' … slightly humbled, it might seem. The through-neck construction was dropped in favor of a more standard, and no doubt simpler, traditional glued-in neck joint, the I and III models now had P-90 pickups, and all in the range carried simpler dot neck inlays. As has so often happened in the evolution of Gibson guitars, the change rendered the original 'reverse-bodied' Firebirds forever after more desirable in the eyes of vintage guitar fanatics.

pickguard (near knobs 1980–86; near edge of body from 1988), jack into top (into side 1980–89; into top from 1991).
Production: 16,677 (1964–70, also see Les Paul Standard 1961–63); 17,394 (1971–79).

1964

Trini Lopez Signature Deluxe (1964–71)
Double-cut archtop, pointed horns, diamond soundholes
- **Body & Hardware:** 16-inch laminated maple hollowbody, double pointed cutaways, Tune-o-matic bridge, trapeze tailpiece with raised diamond, model name on wood tailpiece insert, bound pickguard, triple-bound top and back, Cherry Sunburst finish.
- **Neck:** bound fingerboard and peghead, slashed-diamond inlay, 6-on-a-side tuner arrangement, no peghead ornament.
- **Pickups & Controls:** 2 humbucking pickups, 4 knobs, 3-way pickup selector on treble cutaway bout, standby switch on bass cutaway bout.
Production: 302 (1964–70).

Trini Lopez Signature Standard (1964–71)
Thin double-cut archtop, rounded horns, diamond soundholes
- **Body & Hardware:** 16-inch wide semihollow body of laminated maple, double rounded cutaways, Tune-o-matic bridge, trapeze tailpiece with raised diamond, model name on wood tailpiece insert, laminated beveled-edge pickguard, single-bound top and back, Cherry finish (some with Sparkling Burgundy finish, Pelham Blue).
- **Neck:** bound fingerboard, slashed-diamond inlay, 6-on-a-side tuners, no peghead ornament, decal logo.
- **Pickups & Controls:** 2 humbucking pickups, 4 knobs, selector switch.
Production: 1,966 (1964–70).

1965

ES-335-12 (1965–70): 12-string, double-triangle peghead inlay with rounded points (sharp points from 1968).
Production: 2,062

Firebird I, non-reverse (1965–69)
Solidbody with bass horn larger than treble horn, 1 P-90 pickup
- **Body & Hardware:** bass horn larger than treble horn, wraparound bridge with raised integral saddles, white pickguard with red Firebird logo.
- **Neck:** set neck, unbound rosewood fingerboard, dot inlays, non-beveled peghead. right-angle tuners all on bass side of peghead.
- **Pickups & Controls:** 2 black soapbar P-90 pickups, wraparound bridge with raised integral saddles, white pickguard with red Firebird logo, short-arm vibrato with tubular lever and plastic tip.
Production: 1,590 (1966–69, also some produced in 1965).

Firebird III, non-reverse (1965–69)
Solidbody with bass horn longer than treble horn, 2 P-90 pickups
- **Body & Hardware:** bass horn larger than treble horn, wraparound bridge with raised integral saddles, white pickguard with red Firebird logo, vibrato with tubular arm.
- **Neck:** set neck, unbound rosewood fingerboard, dot inlays, non-beveled peghead, right-angle tuners all on bass side of peghead.
- **Pickups & Controls:** 3 black soapbar P-90 pickups, black sliding selector switch.
Production: 1,535 (1966–69, also some produced in 1965).

Firebird V, non-reverse (1965–69)
Solidbody with bass horn longer than treble horn, 2 mini-humbuckers
- **Body & Hardware:** bass horn larger than treble

CRACKING NECKS AND SHIFTING SPECS

The modernistic double-cutaway design that gave players such excellent access to the upper frets of the SG worked in conjunction with a craze for thin neck profiles in the early 1960s to produce a major neck ache for Gibson, regarding the two-pickup variants of these models in particular. Gibson had already moved the rhythm pickup a little further from the end of the fingerboard than it had been on the Les Paul of 1958–60 in order to provide a little more un-routed wood in the position of this fragile joint, but many models, and SGs in particular, were still proving alarmingly prone to both neck and headstock breaks when dropped.

During the course of the decade Gibson experimented with moving the neck pickup around slightly to improve strength in this area (the different positions are particularly noticeable on 1960s SG Specials), but the maker also sought a couple of other solutions. In late 1965 Gibson reduced the headstock pitch (back angle) from 17 degrees to 14 degrees in an attempt to make this thin joint less prone to breakage. In late 1969 a volute, or thickened wedge, was also added behind the nut for further strength at the region where the neck becomes the headstock. The volute was retained until 1981, although the shallower headstock pitch was returned to its original 17 degrees around 1973, and many players today consider the slightly steeper angle – although only a difference of three degrees – to contribute to a more toneful guitar, thanks to the increased break angle of strings over nut that it creates.

Another altered dimension, although one that had more to do with fashion and feel than strength, was the change of most models' nut widths from 1 11/16 inches to 1 5/8 inches between late 1965 and around 1968. Although a shift of only 1/16-inch, it's enough that most players can readily feel the difference, and those who prefer a little more real estate for fingering at the low end of the fretboard often steer clear of these guitars made between 1966–68.

horn, Tune-o-matic bridge, white pickguard with red Firebird logo, Deluxe vibrato with tubular arm, metal tailpiece cover engraved with Gibson and leaf-and-lyre decoration), nickel-plated hardware.
- **Neck:** set neck, unbound rosewood fingerboard, dot inlays, non-beveled peghead. right-angle tuners all on bass side of peghead.
- **Pickups & Controls:** 2 mini-humbucking pickups with no polepieces, black sliding selector switch.
Production: 492 (1966–69, also some produced in 1965).

Firebird VII, non-reverse (1965–69)
Solidbody with bass horn longer than treble horn, 3 mini-humbuckers
- **Body & Hardware:** bass horn larger than treble

horn, Tune-o-matic bridge, white pickguard with red Firebird logo Deluxe Vibrato with tubular arm, metal tailpiece cover engraved with Gibson and leaf-and-lyre decoration), gold-plated hardware.
- **Neck:** set neck, unbound rosewood fingerboard, dot inlays non-beveled peghead. right-angle tuners all on bass side of peghead.
- **Pickups & Controls:** 3 mini-humbucking pickups with no polepieces, black sliding selector switch.
Production: 283 (1966–69, also some produced in 1965).

1966

ES-125C (1966–70): Pointed cutaway, 1 P-90 pickup. Production: 475.

ES-125CD (1966–70): Pointed cutaway, 2 P-90 pickups. Production: 1,104.

Firebird V 12-string (1966–67): Standard headstock with six tuners per side. Production: 272.

1967

MM-III (1967–71): 3 pickups. Production: 352.

MM-12 (1967–71): 12-string, 2 pickups, no vibrato. Production: 210.

1968

Les Paul Custom (reissue): see earlier entry for Les

Paul Custom 1953.

Les Paul Model (reissue): see earlier entry for Les Paul 1952.

1969

Citation (1969–70, 1975, 1979–83, 1993–current)
Single-cut archtop, fleur de lis on pickguard

- **Body & Hardware:** 17-inch wide, full-depth body, rounded cutaway, solid spruce top, solid maple back and sides, wood pickguard with fleur-de-lis inlay, control knob(s) on pickguard, fancy tailpiece, multiple-bound top and back, gold-plated hardware, varnish (non-lacquer) finish in Sunburst or Natural.
- **Neck:** bound ebony fingerboard with pointed-end, 25½-inch scale, cloud inlay, multiple-bound peghead, fleur-de-lis inlays on front and back of

69

THE LES PAUL RETURNS

A demand for the original Les Paul design that was fueled by the blues-rock boom of the mid and late 1960s inspired Gibson to reissue two versions of the model in 1968. Oddly enough, these took the form of the two-humbucker Les Paul Custom, known as the 'Black Beauty', and the goldtop with P-90s and Tune-o-matic bridge, patterned after the Les Paul circa 1955. Neither was a detail-perfect reproduction, but they fit the bill darn well and helped to satisfy players' cravings for a readily available Les Paul.

The following year, the Les Paul Deluxe with two mini-humbucking pickups was introduced, becoming the 'non-standard Standard' of sorts for many years. Given that the original PAF-style humbucking pickup was a major ingredient in the Les Paul's booming popularity, it remains eternally puzzling that Gibson didn't see fit to release a 'Standard' with these pickups until a range of models returned to the form in the late '70s. Some Deluxes were issued with P-90s and, purportedly, a few were also special-ordered with standard-sized humbuckers, but the mini-humbucker remained far and away the most-seen pickup on the Les Paul of the 1970s (and perhaps the most swapped-out pickup of all time, given the number of players who 'Standardized' their Deluxes). Gibson also played around with the wood formula over the course of the decade, building them for a time with four-piece mahogany/maple-fillet/mahogany/maple-top 'pancake' bodies instead of simply the solid mahogany back and carved maple top, and using a maple neck in place of the traditional mahogany for a time. Regardless, the Deluxe sold well, and if a player was seen with the iconic single-cutaway Gibson solidbody in the 1970s or early '80s, chances are it was one of these variations on the form.

peghead and on bridge.

- **Pickups & Controls:** 1 or 2 floating mini-humbucking pickups (some without visible polepieces), 5-ply maple neck.

Crest (1969–71)
Thinbody double-cut archtop, Brazilian rosewood body

- **Body & Hardware:** 16-inch hollow thinbody archtop body of laminated Brazilian rosewood, double rounded cutaways, flat back (some arched), multiple-bound rosewood pickguard, adjustable rosewood bridge, multiple-bound top, triple-bound back, single-bound *f*-holes, backstripe marquetry, gold-plated (Crest Gold) or silver-plated (Crest Silver) hardware.
- **Neck:** joint at 17th fret, fingerboard raised off of top, block inlays, multiple-bound peghead, 5-piece split-diamond peghead inlay.
- **Pickups & Controls:** 2 floating mini-humbucking pickups.
Production: 162

ES-150DC (1969–74)
Double-cut archtop, full-depth body, rounded horns

- **Body & Hardware:** 16½-inch archtop body of laminated maple, 3-inch deep, Natural, Walnut, or Cherry finish bout.
- **Neck:** rosewood fingerboard, small block inlays, crown peghead inlay.
- **Pickups & Controls:** 2 humbucking pickups, 4 knobs on lower treble bout, master volume knob on upper treble Production: 2,801.

ES-340TD (1969–73)
Same as ES-335 except for maple neck (ES-335 has mahogany neck during ES-340 production period)

- **Body & Hardware:** 16-inch semi-hollowbody of laminated maple, 1⅝-inch deep, double-cutaway, rounded horns, Tune-o-matic bridge, trapeze tailpiece, single-bound top and back, Walnut or Natural finish.
- **Neck:** 3-piece maple neck, single-bound

rosewood fingerboard, small block inlays, crown peghead inlay.
- **Pickups & Controls:** 2 humbucking pickups, 4 knobs, master volume control and master mixer control (rather than 2 volume controls).
Production: 1,561.

Les Paul Deluxe (1969–85, 1992)
Single-cut solidbody, carved top, mini-humbuckers

- **Body & Hardware:** carved maple top, 2-piece mahogany back with maple center laminate (1 piece mahogany from 1977) maple layer in middle, carved maple top cap).
- **Neck:** bound rosewood fingerboard, trapezoid inlays, *Deluxe* on truss-rod cover, *Les Paul* signature and MODEL silkscreened on peghead.
- **Pickups & Controls:** 2 mini-humbucking pickups (some with soapbar pickups).
Production: 2,587 (1970), 35,520 (1971–79 all variations).

Les Paul Jumbo (1969–71)
Single-cut flat-top acoustic, rounded horn, 2 oblong pickups

- **Body & Hardware:** single-cutaway dreadnought size flat-top, rosewood back and sides (catalogued with maple 1971).
- **Neck:** rosewood fingerboard, dot inlays, decal logo.
- **Pickups & Controls:** two oblong low-impedance pickups, 4 knobs.
Production: 139

Les Paul Personal (1969–70)
Single-cut solidbody, carved top, oblong pickups, large block inlays

- **Body & Hardware:** 14-inch wide, single cutaway solidbody, carved top, 3-piece body of mahogany with center maple laminate, contoured back (no contour 1970), Tune-o-matic bridge, Gibson Bigsby vibrato optional, gold-plated hardware, Walnut finish.
- **Neck:** low frets, block inlay (earliest with dot inlay),

CHANGING OWNERSHIP AND THE NORLIN DECLINE

A major portion of Gibson company history had already rolled under the bridge before the electric guitar had even come to be. The first big transition came in the very early days of the company, when founder Orville Gibson sold the rights to the Gibson name and patent to a small group of businessmen in 1902, who subsequently formed the Gibson Mandolin Guitar Manufacturing Company Ltd. The company grew steadily through the first part of the century until guitar production was halted during WWII, and in 1944 was sold again to the massive Chicago Musical Instrument Company (CMI), which continued to cultivate the Gibson brand as one of the leading stringed instrument manufacturers in the world.

The next, and perhaps most infamous, change of ownership came in December of 1969, when Gibson was acquired by Ecuadorian Company Limited (ECL). The company changed its name to Norlin just a few months later, using the first three letters from ECL chairman Norman Stevens's name and the last three from that of CMI head M.H. Berlin. For many players and collectors, Norlin's ownership – which lasted from late 1969 to early 1986 – was to Gibson what CBS's was to Fender, and marks an era of rationalized production from a parent company perceived as unsympathetic to the craft and nuance of musical instrument manufacturing. Gibson continued to be a major name in the guitar industry under Norlin, but aspects of instrument manufacture under the conglomerate – from the conception of new models, to the standards of existing favorites, to the quality control of the entire production range – are considered by many to represent a dark period in Gibson history. Many models of the late 1970s and early '80s – various Limited Edition and 'custom made' Les Pauls in particular – reclaim a measure of the CMI glory years, and certainly plenty of others are perfectly playable utilitarian guitars but, on the whole, Norlin-era guitars are not the most admired of Gibsons.

5-piece split-diamond peghead inlay.
- **Pickups & Controls:** 2 oblong low-impedance pickups mounted at a slant, *Gibson* embossed on pickup covers, microphone input jack on side of upper bass bout, mic volume control knob and 1 switch on upper bass bout, guitar input jack on side of lower treble bout, 4 knobs and 2 slide switches on lower treble bout, Tune-o-matic bridge.

Production: 370.

Les Paul Professional (1969–70)
Single-cut solidbody, carved top, oblong pickups, trapezoid inlays
- **Body & Hardware:** 14-inch wide, single cutaway solidbody, carved top, 3-piece body of mahogany with center maple laminate, contoured back (no

contour 1970), Tune-o-matic bridge, Gibson Bigsby tailpiece optional, , chrome-plated hardware, Walnut finish.
- **Neck:** rosewood fingerboard, trapezoid inlay.
- **Pickups & Controls:** 2 oblong low-impedance pickups mounted at a slant, *Gibson* embossed on pickup covers, pickup selector switch on upper bass bout, 4 knobs, slide switch for in/out phase, 3-position slide switch for tone, 3-prong jack.

Production: 901.

1970-71

ES-320TD (1971–74)
Thinbody double-cut archtop, dot inlays, oblong pickups

- **Body & Hardware:** 16-inch double cutaway thinbody of laminated maple, Tune-o-matic bridge, nickel-plated bridge cover with logo, black plastic pickguard, bound top and back (black-painted edges to simulate binding on Natural finish models), Natural, Walnut, or Cherry finish.
- **Neck:** rosewood fingerboard, dot inlays, decal logo.
- **Pickups & Controls:** 2 Melody Maker pickups with embossed Gibson logo, oblong metal control plate with 2 knobs and 2 slide switches.
Production: 664.

Firebird (V) (1972–73): *LE* limited edition medallion, logo embossed on pickup covers. Production: 366.

Howard Roberts Custom (1970, 1974–80)
Single-cut archtop, oval soundhole
- **Body & Hardware:** 16-inch wide, full-depth body, pointed cutaway, laminated maple top, oval hole, height-adjustable ebony bridge, multiple-bound pickguard, multiple-bound top and back, chrome-plated hardware, (some labeled Howard Roberts Artist, 1974–76).
- **Neck:** bound ebony fingerboard (rosewood from 1974), slotted-block inlays, multiple-bound peghead, vine-pattern peghead inlay.
- **Pickups & Controls:** 1 floating humbucking pickup.
Production: 1,152.

Howard Roberts DE (1970): 2 pickups. Production: 2.

Howard Roberts Standard Electric (1970): Bound rosewood fingerboard, slotted-block inlays, vertical oval peghead inlay, 1 floating mini-humbucking pickup. Production: 3.

Les Paul Custom '54 (1972): Reissue of 1954 Les Paul Custom, Alnico V neck pickup, P-90 bridge pickup, standard 6-digit serial number with *LE* prefix.

Les Paul Custom/3 pickups (1971–73, 1976, 1978): 3 pickups.

Les Paul Recording (1971–79)
Single-cut solidbody, carved top, oblong pickups, small block inlays
- 13½-inch wide, single cutaway solidbody, carved top, Tune-o-matic bridge.
- **Neck:** bound rosewood fingerboard, small block inlays, 5-piece split-diamond peghead inlay.
- **Pickups & Controls:** 2 oblong low-impedance pickups mounted at a slant with embossed *Gibson*, 4 knobs (volume, treble, bass, "decade" tone control) and pickup selector on control plate, high/low impedance selector switch (transformer built into guitar), 3-way tone control and 2-way phase control on control plate, jack on top into control plate.
Production: 5,380.

Les Paul Standard '58 (1971–73): Similar to 1954 Les Paul Model, 2 soapbar pickups with *Gibson* embossed on covers, wraparound bridge/tailpiece, 1-piece neck with no volute, gold-top finish. Production: 1,077.

SG Deluxe (1971–72, 1981–84, 1998–2000)
Double-cut solidbody, pointed horns, semi-circular control plate or 3 Firebird mini-humbuckers
- Body & Hardware: solid mahogany double-cutaway body, pointed horns, non-beveled cutaways, triangular Les Paul Standard-style pickguard flush with top (large SG-style pickup from 1981), Tune-o-matic bridge (large rectangular base 1981–84), Gibson Bigsby vibrato (no vibrato 1998, Maestro Bigsby-style from 1999), Natural, Cherry or Walnut finish (Ebony, Ice Blue or Hellfire Red 1998–2000).
- **Neck:** bound rosewood fingerboard (unbound ebony from 1998), small block inlay (some with dots 1971–84, all with dots 1998–2000), decal logo.

- **Pickups & Controls:** 2 humbucking pickups (3 Firebird-style mini-humbucking pickups with no polepieces from 1988)), 4 knobs (2 knobs, 6-way rotary switch 1998–2000), semi-circular control plate (no control plate from 1998).
Production: 7,615.

SG Pro (1971, 1973–74)
Double-cut solidbody, pointed horns, 2 P-90s, semi-circular control plate

- **Body & Hardware:** double-cutaway solid mahogany body, pointed horns, wing-shaped pickguard (Les Paul Standard-style) mounted on top, Tune-o-matic bridge with rectangular base, Gibson Bigsby vibrato, Cherry, Walnut or Natural Mahogany finish.
- **Neck:** single-bound rosewood fingerboard, dot inlays, pearl logo.
- **Pickups & Controls:** 2 black soapbar P-90 pickups with mounting rings, semi-circular control plate.
Production: 2,995.

SG-100 (1971)
Double-cut solidbody, pointed horns, oblong pickup, oblong control plate

- **Body & Hardware:** double cutaway with pointed horns, solid poplar body (some mahogany), metal bridge cover with engraved *Gibson*, some with triangular Les Paul-type pickguard, some with large SG-type pickguard, Cherry or Walnut.
- **Neck:** unbound rosewood fingerboard, dot inlays, standard Gibson peghead shape.
- **Pickups & Controls:** oblong Melody Maker type pickup, large pickup mounting plate, oblong control plate.
Production: 1,229.

SG-200 (1971): 2 pickups, 2 slide switches, Cherry, Walnut or black finish. Production: 2,980.

SG-250 (1971): 2 pickups, 2 slide switches, Cherry Sunburst finish. Production: 527.

1972

ES-325TD (1972–79)
Thinbody double-cut archtop, 1 f-hole

- **Body & Hardware:** 16-inch semihollow archtop, Tune-o-matic bridge, trapeze tailpiece with pointed ends, single-bound top and back.
- **Neck:** rosewood fingerboard, dot inlays.
- **Pickups & Controls:** 2 mini-humbucking pickups with no visible poles (polepieces from 1976), semi-circular plastic control plate, 4 knobs.
Production: 2,445.

SG I (1972–73)
Double-cut solidbody, pointed horns, black mini-humbuckers

- **Body & Hardware:** double cutaway with pointed horns, beveled edges, mahogany body, triangular wing-shaped pickguard, wraparound bridge/tailpiece, Cherry or Walnut finish.
- **Neck:** dot inlays standard Gibson peghead shape.
- **Pickups & Controls:** black plastic-covered mini-humbucking pickup with no poles, 2 knobs, semi-circular control plate.
Production: 2,331.

SG I with Junior pickup (1972): P-90 pickup.
Production: 61.

SG II (1972): 2 pickups, 2 knobs, 2 slide switches, Cherry or Walnut finish.
Production: 2,927.

SG III (1972–73): 2 pickups, 2 slide switches, Tune-o-matic bridge, Cherry Sunburst finish.
Production: 953.

SG-100 Junior (1972): P-90 pickup.
Production: 272.

HIT AND MISS MODELS (MOSTLY MISS)

Like many guitar manufacturers, in the late 1970s and early '80s, Gibson struggled to find a foothold in a music world more and more dominated by electronics – and by synthesizer-based keyboards in particular – and consequently threw out a lot of oddball and generally 'modernistic' designs that just didn't stick (and no, they didn't become classics a decade down the road either, unlike the Flying V and Explorer of the Modernistic Series launched in 1958). Ironically, the first raft of ill-received Gibson electrics of the era came early on, in 1969, with the return of the namesake of Gibson's most legendary model.

Upon re-signing his endorsement deal with Gibson, Les Paul had urged the company to issue models that incorporated the low-impedance pickups that Paul had long favored himself. These appeared in 1969 as the Les Paul Personal and Professional models, which were replaced by the similar Les Paul Recording model in 1971. The models were generally considered ugly, their controls confusing, and they never found favor with musicians, in their day or after. The final incarnation of these remained in the catalog until 1979. The semi-acoustic Les Paul Signature of 1973 didn't fare much better (although most felt the guitar at least looked a little better than its siblings), nor did the original low-impedance L-5S, nor indeed the version with standard high-impedance humbuckers that followed it. Other dodos of the era were the L-6S, bolt-neck Marauder and S-1, laminated-bodied V-II, active-electronics-equipped RD Series, wood-and-plastic bodied Sonex 180, and pig-ugly Corvus. That said, some of these 'clunkers' didn't do too badly: Gibson sold more than 7,000 Marauders between 1975–'79, and more than 3,000 S-1s over a similar time frame.

1973

Les Paul Signature (1973–77)
Thinbody double-cut archtop, asymmetrical body, oblong pickups

- **Body & Hardware:** 16-inch wide, thin body, rounded bass-side horn, more pointed treble-side cutaway, large rectangular Tune-o-matic bridge, Sunburst or gold finish.
- **Neck:** bound rosewood fingerboard, trapezoid inlay.
- **Pickups & Controls:** 2 oblong low-impedance humbucking pickups with white covers (rectangular pickups with embossed *Gibson* from 1974, high/low impedance humbuckers from 1976), 4 knobs (volume, treble tone, midrange tone, in/out phase switch), 3-way selector on upper bass bout, 2 jacks (high impedance on top, low-impedance on rim).
Production: 1,453.

L-5S (1973–84)
Single-cut solidbody, flowerpot peghead inlay

- **Body & Hardware:** 13½-inch wide, single cutaway, carved maple top, contoured back, large rectangular Tune-o-matic bridge, large L-5 style plate tailpiece with silver center insert (stopbar from 1975, TP-6 from 1978), no pickguard, 7-ply top binding and 3-ply back binding with black line on side, maple control cavity cover, gold-plated hardware, Natural, Cherry Sunburst or Vintage Sunburst finish.
- **Neck:** 5-piece maple/mahogany neck, 24¾-inch scale, 17 frets clear of body, bound ebony fingerboard with pointed end, abalone block inlays, 5-ply fingerboard binding with black line on side, 22 frets, 5-ply peghead binding, flowerpot peghead inlay.
- **Pickups & Controls:** 2 large oblong low-impedance pickups with metal covers and

embossed logo (humbuckers from 1974), 4 knobs.
Production: 1,813 (1973–79).

L-6S / L6-S Custom: (1973–75 L-6S; 1975–79 L-6S Custom)

Single-cut solidbody, narrow peghead
- **Body & Hardware:** 13½-inch wide, 1⅛-inch deep, single cutaway, maple body, large rectangular Tune-o-matic bridge, stop tailpiece.
- **Neck:** unbound maple fingerboard with Natural finish, unbound ebony fingerboard with Tobacco Sunburst finish, small block inlay (dots from 1975), 24 frets, 18 frets clear of body, 24¾-inch scale, narrow peghead with similar shape to snakehead L-5 of late 1920s.
- **Pickups & Controls:** 2 5-sided humbucking pickups with no polepieces (rectangular from 1975), 3 knobs (volume, midrange and tone), 6-position rotary tone selector switch for parallel and phase selection, chrome-plated hardware, Natural or Cherry finish.
Production: 12,460.

L-5CES Custom (1973–77)

Single-cut archtop, 2 pickups, 6-finger tailpiece
- **Body & Hardware:** 17-inch wide maple body, rounded cutaway, solid carved spruce top single-bound *f*-holes, multiple-bound top and back, TP-6 6-finger tailpiece.
- **Neck:** ebony fingerboard, split-block inlays, 5-piece split-diamond headstock inlay, multiple-bound headstock.
- **Pickups & Controls:** 2 humbucking pickups, 4 knobs.
Production: 17 (1973–77), 124 (1978–79)

1974-75

Les Paul Custom 20th Anniversary (1974): All Les Paul Customs in 1974 have *Twentieth Anniversary* engraved in block letters on the 15th-fret inlay, black or white finish.

Les Paul Custom/maple fingerboard (1975–81): Maple fingerboard, Ebony or Natural finish.

Les Paul Deluxe BB (1975–77): Blue sparkle top finish.

Les Paul Deluxe RR (1975): Red sparkle top finish.

Les Paul 55 (1974–80)

Single-cut solidbody, Les Paul Special features, 2 P-90 pickups, "Les Paul Model" on silkscreen
- **Body & Hardware:** single cutaway, slab mahogany body, Tune-o-matic bridge (earliest with wraparound bridge/tailpiece).
- **Neck:** mahogany, bound rosewood fingerboard, dot inlays, plastic keystone tuner buttons, *Les Paul Model* on peghead, pearl logo.
- **Pickups & Controls:** 2 black soapbar P-90 pickups, 4 knobs.
Production: 2,775 (1974–79).

L-6S Deluxe (1975–80)

Single-cut solidbody, strings through body, 5-sided pickups
- **Body & Hardware:** 13½-inch wide, 1⅛-inch deep, single cutaway, maple body, beveled top around bass side, large rectangular Tune-o-matic bridge, strings anchor through body, string holes on a line diagonal to strings.
- **Neck:** unbound rosewood fingerboard, small block inlay (dots from 1978), metal tuner buttons.
- **Pickups & Controls:** 2 5-sided humbucking pickups with black covers, 3 screws in pickup mounting rings, 2 knobs, 3-way pickup selector switch.
Production: 3,483 (1975–79).

Marauder (1975–81)

Single-cut solidbody, humbucker and blade pickups
- **Body & Hardware:** 12½-inch wide, Les Paul-shape single cutaway, maple or mahogany body, large pickguard covers entire upper body and extends around lower treble bout.

- **Neck:** bolt-on maple neck, unbound rosewood fingerboard (maple from 1978), dot inlays, triangular peghead with rounded top, decal logo.
- **Pickups & Controls:** humbucking pickup in neck position, blade pickup in bridge position, pickups set in clear epoxy, 2 knobs, rotary tone selector switch between knobs (some with switch on cutaway bout, 1978).

Production: 7,029 (1975–79).

Midnight Special (1974–79)
Thin single-cut solidbody, 2 humbuckers with no polepieces

- **Body & Hardware:** solid maple body, single-cutaway, non-beveled top around bass side, large rectangular Tune-o-matic bridge, strings anchor through body on a diagonal line, chrome-plated hardware.
- **Neck:** bolt-on maple neck, maple fingerboard, decal logo, metal tuner buttons.
- **Pickups & Controls:** 2 humbucking pickups with metal covers and no polepieces, 2 knobs, 2-way tone switch, jack into top.

Production: 2,077.

Strings and Things Reissue (1975–78): Special order by Strings and Things, Gibson dealer in Memphis, Tennessee, curly top, uniform-depth binding in cutaway. Production: 28

SG III with humbuckers (1975): Humbucking pickups. Production: 61.

1976

ES-175T (1976–79): Thinbody 1⅞-inch deep. Production: 1,063.

The Explorer / Explorer CM (1976, 1981–84)
Angular solidbody, curly maple top, fine-tune tailpiece

- **Body & Hardware:** angular maple solidbody, bound curly maple top, Tune-o-matic bridge, TP-6 fine-tune tailpiece, gold-plated hardware, Antique Sunburst, Vintage Cherry Sunburst or Antique Natural finish.
- **Neck:** maple, unbound ebony fingerboard, dot inlays, some with *E/2* on truss-rod cover, pearl logo.
- **Pickups & Controls:** 2 exposed-coil Dirty Fingers humbucking pickups, 3 knobs in straight line, knobs mounted into top, 3-way selector switch on upper treble horn.

Firebird 76 (1976–78)
Solidbody with treble horn longer than bass horn, Firebird with stars on pickguard

- **Body & Hardware:** reverse body, Tune-o-matic bridge, red-and-blue Bicentennial Firebird figure (with stars) on pickguard near switch, gold-plated hardware, Sunburst, Natural mahogany, white or Ebony finish.
- **Neck:** neck-through-body, unbound rosewood fingerboard, dot inlays, straight-through banjo tuners with metal buttons.
- **Pickups & Controls:** 2 mini-humbucking pickups, 4 knobs, selector switch.

Production: 2,847.

Howard Roberts Artist (1976–80): Ebony fingerboard, gold-plated hardware. Production: 129.

The Les Paul (1976–79)
Single-cut solidbody, carved flamed maple top, wood knobs and pickups covers

- **Body & Hardware:** carved maple top, maple back, Tune-o-matic bridge (larger rectangular bridge from 1978), stopbar tailpiece (TP-6 fine tune from 1978) rosewood pickguard, rosewood control plates on back, rosewood outer binding, green- and red-stained wood inner bindings, gold-plated hardware, Natural or Rosewood finish.
- **Neck:** maple, 3-piece ebony-rosewood-ebony fingerboard, abalone block inlays, 5-piece split-diamond peghead inlay, pearl tuner buttons, pearl

GOIN' SOUTH

Whatever players and collectors might think of Norlin-era Gibsons today, the guitars were selling well in the early 1970s, and the boom required further expansion of Gibson's manufacturing facilities. The troublesome labor disputes of the early 1970s inspired Norlin to attain this increased capacity by building a new 100,000 square foot factory in Nashville, TN, which opened in the summer of 1975. Over the course of the next few years Gibson's general production was weighted more and more toward Nashville, and by the late 1970s and early '80s the Kalamazoo factory was largely relegated to custom and limited instruments, such as the Les Paul Heritage 80, Flying V and Explorer.

Gibson ceased production at Kalamazoo entirely in June 1984, and relocated the company's corporate and manufacturing structures to Nashville. Between the opening of the Nashville plant and the closure of the Kalamazoo plant, Norlin reported pretax losses attributable to its holdings in the musical instrument industry of $145 million, and it appeared by the mid 1980s that Gibson was plummeting toward out-and-out closure and liquidation.

Meanwhile, three former Gibson managers – Jim Deurloo, Marv Lam, and J.P. Moats – had refused to make the journey south, leased part of the former Gibson factory in Kalamazoo, and formed the Heritage guitar company in April 1985.

76

plate on back of peghead with limited edition number.
- **Pickups & Controls:** 2 super humbucking pickups, 5-sided rosewood pickup covers, rosewood knobs and switch tip.

Production: 73.

Les Paul Artisan (1976–1981)
Single-cut solidbody, carved top, hearts-and-flowers (banjo-style) inlays
- **Body & Hardware:** carved maple top, Tune-o-matic bridge (larger rectangular bridge from 1980), TP-6 tailpiece, Walnut, Tobacco Sunburst, or Ebony finish.
- **Neck:** single-bound ebony fingerboard, multiple-bound peghead, hearts-and-flowers inlay on fingerboard and peghead, pearl logo in thin pre-war style script, gold-plated hardware.
- **Pickups & Controls:** 2 humbucking pickups (3 pickups optional, 1976–78; 3 pickups standard from 1979).

Production: 2,220 (1976–79).

Les Paul Custom/nickel-plated parts (1976, 1979–86, 1996): Nickel-plated hardware (chrome 1985–86), 2 humbucking pickups (3 pickups 1996).

Les Paul Special Double Cutaway (1976, 1978–85, 1993–94): Double cutaway, Tune-o-matic bridge (wraparound 1993–94), selector switch on treble side near bridge, chrome-plated hardware (nickel-plated 1993–94) metal tuner buttons, *Les Paul Model* on peghead.

Marauder Custom (1976–77): 3-way selector switch on cutaway bout, bound fingerboard, block inlays, Tobacco Sunburst finish.
Production: 83.

S-1 (1976–79)
Thin single-cut solidbody, 3 pickups
- **Body & Hardware:** 12½-inch wide, Les Paul-shape single cutaway, rectangular Tune-o-matic bridge, stop tailpiece, large pickguard covers entire upper body and extends around lower treble bout.

- **Neck:** bolt-on neck, maple fingerboard (some early with rosewood), dot inlays, triangular peghead with rounded top.
- **Pickups & Controls:** 3 single-coil pickups with center bar, pickups set in clear epoxy (black pickup covers from 1978), 2-way toggle on cutaway bout (selects bridge pickup alone), 4-position rotary switch for pickup selection, 2 knobs (volume, tone).
Production: 3,089.

1977

ES-240 (1977–1978)
Thinbody double-cut archtop, rounded horns, same as ES-335 but with coil-tap switch
- **Body & Hardware:** thindouble-cutaway semi-hollowbody, rounded horns, Tune-o-matic bridge, stopbar tailpiece.
- **Neck:** bound rosewood fingerboard, small block inlays, crown peghead inlay, pearl logo.
- **Pickups & Controls:** 2 humbucking pickups, 4 knobs, selector switch, coil-tap switch on lower bass treble bout near tone and volume knobs.
Production: 3.

Les Paul Custom 25th Anniversary (1977): *25th Anniversary* engraved in script on tailpiece, *Les Paul* signature on pickguard, chrome-plated hardware, silver metallic finish.

Melody Maker Double 2nd version (1977–83): Rounded horns, horns point away from neck, 2 pickups, Tune-o-matic bridge (earliest with stud-mounted wraparound bridge/tailpiece), 4 knobs, earliest with bolt-on neck, narrow peghead, metal tuner buttons, Cherry or Sunburst finish.
Production: 1,085 (1977–79).

RD Custom (1977–78) / **77 Custom** (1979)
Solidbody with longer treble horn, maple fingerboard
- **Body & Hardware:** double cutaway, 14⅝-inch

wide, upper treble horn longer than upper bass horn, lower bass horn larger than lower treble horn, Tune-o-matic bridge, chrome-plated hardware, large backplate, Natural or Walnut finish.
- **Neck:** 25½-inch scale, maple fingerboard, dot inlays, model name on truss-rod cover, decal logo.
- **Pickups & Controls:** 2 humbucking pickups, active electronics, 4 knobs (standard Gibson controls), 3-way pickup selector switch, 2-way mini switch for mode selection (neutral or bright).
Production: 1,498 (1977–79).

RD Standard (1977–1978)
Solidbody with longer treble horn, dot inlays, 2 humbuckers
- **Body & Hardware:** double cutaway, 14⅝-inch wide, upper treble horn longer than upper bass horn, lower bass horn larger than lower treble horn, Tune-o-matic bridge, chrome-plated hardware, Natural, Tobacco Sunburst or Walnut finish.
- **Neck:** 25½-inch scale, rosewood fingerboard, dot inlays, model name on truss-rod cover, decal logo.
- **Pickups & Controls:** 2 humbucking pickups, 4 knobs, 1 selector switch.

1978

ES-175CC (1978–79): Charlie Christian pickup, 3 screws into top, adjustable rosewood bridge, Sunburst or Walnut stain finish.
Production: 489.

ES-347TD (1978–85) / **ES-347S** (1987–93)
Thinbody double-cut archtop, 2 humbuckers, TP-6 tailpiece
- **Body & Hardware:** 16-inch semi-hollow body of laminated maple, 1⅝-inch deep, double rounded cutaways, Tune-o-matic bridge, TP-6 fine-tune tailpiece, laminated beveled-edge pickguard,

single-bound top and back, chrome-plated hardware (gold-plated from 1987).
- **Neck:** bound ebony fingerboard, large block inlays, bound peghead (multiply binding from 1987), crown peghead inlay, pearl logo.
- **Pickups & Controls:** 2 humbucking pickups, 4 knobs and 1 pickup selector switch on lower treble bout, coil-tap switch on upper treble bout.
Production: 1,896 (1978–79).

Jimmy Wallace Reissue (1978–97): *Jimmy Wallace* on truss-rod cover, special order by musician/dealer Jimmy Wallace of Sunnyvale, Texas.

Kalamazoo Award (1978–84)
Single-cut archtop, flying bird inlay on peghead
- **Body & Hardware:** 17-inch wide, full-depth body, carved spruce top, maple back and side, adjustable ebony bridge with pearl inlays, wood pickguard with abalone inlay, knobs mounted on pickguard, multiple-bound top and back, bound *f*-holes, gold-plated hardware, Sunburst or Natural varnish (non-lacquer) finish.
- **Neck:** bound ebony fingerboard, abalone block inlays, multiple-bound peghead, flying bird peghead inlay.
- **Pickups & Controls:** 1 floating mini-humbucking pickup (some without visible polepieces).

Les Paul North Star (1978)
Single-cut solidbody, carved top, star on peghead
- Carved maple top, mahogany back, multiple-bound top.
- Neck: single-bound fingerboard, trapezoid inlays, star peghead inlay, *North Star* on truss-rod cover.
- **Pickups & Controls:** 2 humbucking pickups, 4 knobs, selector switch on upper bass bout.

Les Paul Pro-Deluxe (1978–81)
Single-cut solidbody, carved top, ebony fingerboard, 2 P-90s
- **Body & Hardware:** carved maple top, Tune-o-matic bridge, cream binding, chrome-plated

hardware, gold-top, Ebony, Tobacco Sunburst or Cherry Sunburst finish.
- **Neck:** ebony fingerboard, trapezoid inlays, Schaller tuners.
- **Pickups & Controls:** 2 soapbar P-90 pickups, 4 knobs, selector switch on upper bass bout.
Production: 1,416.

SG Studio (1978)
Double-cut solidbody, pointed horns, bound fingerboard, dot inlays, 2 humbuckers
- **Body & Hardware:** solid mahogany double-cutaway body, pointed horns, no pickguard, some with satin finish.
- **Neck:** bound rosewood fingerboard, dot inlays.
- **Pickups & Controls:** 2 humbucking pickups, 3 knobs, 1 toggle switch.
Production: 931.

The Paul (Standard) (1978–81) / **Firebrand Les Paul** (1981)
Thin single-cut solidbody, walnut body
- **Body & Hardware:** thinsingle-cutaway solidbody, walnut body, Tune-o-matic bridge.
- **Neck:** walnut neck, unbound ebony fingerboard, dot inlays, decal logo (routed logo with no inlay or hot-branded logo, 1981).
- **Pickups & Controls:** 2 exposed-coil humbucking pickups, selector switch near control knobs, no pickguard.

1979

ES-Artist (1979–85)
Thinbody double-cut archtop, winged-f peghead inlay
- **Body & Hardware:** 16-inch semi-hollow archtop body of laminated maple, 1¾-inch deep, no *f*-holes, Tune-o-matic bridge, TP-6 tailpiece, laminated beveled-edge pickguard, multiple-bound top and back, gold-plated hardware, Cherry Sunburst, Ebony or Antique Fireburst finish.

79

- **Neck:** single-bound ebony fingerboard, off-center dot inlay near bass edge of fingerboard, pearl logo.
- **Pickups & Controls:** 2 humbucking pickups, active electronics, 3 knobs (bass, treble, volume), 3-way selector switch, 3 mini-toggle switches (bright, compression/expansion, active on/off).

ES-335 CRR (1979): Country Rock Regular, 2 exposed-coil Dirty Fingers humbuckers, coil tap, brass nut, Antique Sunburst finish.
Production: 300

ES-335 CRRS (1979): Country Rock Stereo, stereo electronics, master volume control, coil tap, TP-6 fine-tune tailpiece, brass nut, Country Tobacco or Dixie Brown (pink-to-brown Sunburst) finish.
Production: 300

ES-335 Pro (1979–81): 2 Dirty Fingers humbucking pickups with exposed coils.

Explorer II (1979–83)
Angular multi-layer solidbody with beveled edges
- **Body & Hardware:** 5-layer walnut and maple body with walnut or maple top, beveled body edges, Tune-o-matic bridge, TP-6 tailpiece, gold-plated hardware, Natural finish.
- **Neck:** 22 frets, 24-inch ¾-scale, unbound ebony fingerboard, dot inlays, *E/2* on truss-rod cover.
- **Pickups & Controls:** 2 humbucking pickups with exposed coils, 3 knobs in straight line, knobs mounted into top, 3-way selector switch into pickguard on upper treble horn.

Flying V II (1979–82)
V-shaped layered body, boomerang pickups
- **Body & Hardware:** 5-layer maple/walnut body with walnut or maple top, beveled top and back body edges, Tune-o-matic bridge, gold-plated hardware, Natural finish.
- **Neck:** unbound ebony fingerboard, dot inlays.
- **Pickups & Controls:** 2 boomerang-shaped pickups.

GK-55 (1979–80)
Les Paul shape, bolt-on neck, TP-6 tailpiece
- **Body & Hardware:** single cutaway mahogany solidbody, flat top, rectangular tune-o-matic bridge, TP-6 tailpiece or stop tailpiece, no pickguard, Tobacco Sunburst finish.
- **Neck:** bolt-on neck, unbound rosewood fingerboard, dot inlays, model name on truss-rod cover, decal logo.
- **Pickups & Controls:** 2 Dirty Fingers pickups with exposed coils, 4 knobs.
Production: 1,000.

Howard Roberts Artist Double Pickup (1979–80): 2 pickups, bridge pickup mounted into top with mounting ring.

Howard Roberts Fusion (1979–1990) / **Howard Roberts Fusion II** (1988–90) / **Howard Roberts Fusion III** (1991–current)
Thin single-cut archtop, pointed horn, wider cutaway than other models
- **Body & Hardware:** 14⅞-inch wide, semi-hollowbody, 2⁵⁄₁₆-inch deep, cutaway shape similar to Les Paul solidbody models, Tune-o-matic bridge, TP-6 tailpiece (6-finger from 1990), triple-bound top, bound back, , chrome-plated hardware (gold-plated from 1991).
- **Neck:** Dot inlays crown peghead inlay, Sunburst, Fireburst, or Ebony finish.
- **Pickups & Controls:** 2 humbucking pickups, 4 knobs.

Les Paul Kalamazoo (1979)
Single cut solidbody, carved top, KM on truss-rod cover
- **Body & Hardware:** single-cutaway solidbody, carved 2-piece maple top, large rectangular Tune-o-matic bridge, stop tailpiece, examples from first run with *Custom Made* plate nailed onto top below tailpiece, Antique Sunburst, Natural or Cherry Sunburst finish.
- **Neck:** bound rosewood fingerboard, pearl

'79

trapezoid inlays, *Les Paul KM* on truss-rod cover.

- **Pickups & Controls:** 2 exposed-coil humbucking pickups with cream-colored coils, 4 speed knobs, selector switch on upper bass bout.

Production: 1,500.

Les Paul Special Double CMT (1979): Double-cutaway, curly maple top.

Production: 133.

L.P. Artist (Les Paul Artist, Les Paul Active) (1979–81)

Single-cut solidbody, carved top, LP on peghead

- **Body & Hardware:** single cutaway, carved maple top, Tune-o-matic bridge, TP-6 fine-tune tailpiece, multiple-bound top, gold-plated hardware.
- **Neck:** bound ebony fingerboard, large block inlays, brass nut, triple-bound peghead, script *LP* peghead inlay.
- **Pickups & Controls:** 2 humbucking pickups (3 pickups optional), active electronics, 3 knobs (volume, treble, bass), 3 mini switches (expansion, compression, brightness).

Production: 230 (1979).

RD Artist/79 (1979–80) **/ RD** (1981)

Solidbody with longer treble horn, winged-f on peghead

- Double cutaway, 14⅝-inch wide, upper treble horn longer than upper bass horn, lower bass horn larger than lower treble horn, Tune-o-matic bridge, TP-6 tailpiece, large backplate, gold-plated hardware.
- **Neck:** 3-piece mahogany neck, 24¾-inch scale, bound ebony fingerboard (some unbound), block inlays, multiple-bound peghead, winged-*f* peghead inlay, pearl logo.
- **Pickups & Controls:** 2 humbucking pickups, active electronics, 4 knobs (standard Gibson controls), 3-way pickup selector switch, 3-way switch for mode selection (neutral, bright, front pickup expansion with back pickup compression.

Production: 2,340 (1977–79).

The SG (1979–80) / **SG Standard** (1981)

Double-cut solidbody, pointed horns, walnut body, exposed-coil pickups

- **Body & Hardware:** double-cutaway walnut solidbody, pointed horns, Tune-o-matic bridge, small pickguard, chrome-plated hardware, Natural finish.
- **Neck:** walnut neck, ebony fingerboard, dot inlays, decal logo or routed logo with no inlay ("Firebrand" branded logo 1980, pearl logo 1981).
- **Pickups & Controls:** 1 standard humbucking pickup, 1 Super humbucking "velvet brick" pickup, no pickup covers, 4 knobs.

The SG / The SG Deluxe (1979–84)

Double-cut solidbody, pointed horns, exposed-coil pickups

- **Body & Hardware:** solid mahogany double-cutaway body, pointed horns, Tune-o-matic bridge, small pickguard.
- **Neck:** walnut neck, ebony fingerboard, dot inlays, chrome-plated hardware.
- **Pickups & Controls:** 1 standard humbucking pickup, 1 Super humbucking "velvet brick" pickup, no pickup covers, black mounting rings, 4 knobs.

SG Exclusive (1979)

Double-cut solidbody, pointed horns, block inlays, rotary coil-tap control

- **Body & Hardware:** solid mahogany double-cutaway body, pointed horns, white pickguard, Ebony finish.
- **Neck:** bound rosewood fingerboard, block inlays, pearl logo, crown peghead inlay.
- **Pickups & Controls:** 2 humbucking pickups with or without covers, coil tap controlled by rotary knob (in standard volume knob position).

Production: 478.

1980

B.B. King Standard (1980) / **Lucille Standard** (1981–85)

Thinbody double-cut archtop, no f-holes, dot inlays, Lucille on peghead

- **Body & Hardware:** thindouble-cutaway semi-hollowbody of laminated maple, no f-holes, Nashville Tune-o-matic bridge, TP-6 tailpiece, laminated beveled-edge pickguard, multiple-bound top and back, chrome-plated hardware, Ebony or Cherry finish.
- **Neck:** single-bound rosewood fingerboard, dot inlays, *Lucille* peghead inlay.
- **Pickups & Controls:** 2 PAF humbucking pickups, stereo electronics with 2 jacks.

B.B. King Custom (1980) / **Lucille** (1981–85) / **B.B. King Lucille** (1986–current)

Thinbody double-cut archtop, no f-holes, block inlays, Lucille on peghead

- **Body & Hardware:** thin double-cutaway semi-hollowbody of laminated maple, no f-holes, TP-6 tailpiece, multiple-bound top and back, single-bound pickguard, Tune-o-matic bridge, gold-plated hardware, Ebony or Cherry finish.
- **Neck:** bound ebony fingerboard, large block inlays, *Lucille* peghead inlay.
- **Pickups & Controls:** 2 PAF humbucking pickups, Vari-tone rotary tone selector switch, stereo wiring with 2 jacks.

Firebird (1980): 1-piece neck-through-body, unbound rosewood fingerboard, dot inlays, Cherry, Ebony or Natural finish.

KZ-II (1980–81)

Double-cut solidbody, rounded horns (different from Les Pauls), 2 humbuckers

- **Body & Hardware:** double-cutaway solidbody, with Melody Maker style rounded horns, made in Kalamazoo factory, Tune-o-matic bridge, chrome-plated hardware, Walnut stain with satin non-gloss finish.
- **Neck:** dot inlays metal tuner buttons, standard Gibson peghead size, *KZ-II* on truss-rod cover.
- **Pickups & Controls:** 2 humbucking pickups.

Les Paul Heritage 80 (1980–82)

Single-cut solidbody, carved top, Heritage 80 on truss-rod cover

- **Body & Hardware:** 2-piece highly flamed maple top, binding inside cutaway same depth as rest of top binding, nickel-plated hardware.
- **Neck:** 3-piece neck, *Heritage 80* on truss-rod cover, earliest with 4-digit serial number (0001, 0002, etc.), small peghead.
- **Pickups & Controls:** 2 humbucking pickups, 4 knobs, selector switch on upper bass bout.

Les Paul Heritage 80 Elite (1980–82): 1-piece neck, ebony fingerboard, *Heritage 80 Elite* on truss-rod cover, chrome-plated hardware.

Les Paul Heritage 80 Award: 1-piece mahogany neck, ebony fingerboard, pearl trapezoid inlays, gold-plated hardware, oval pearl medallion on back of peghead with limited edition number: 1981.

Les Paul K-II (1980)

Double-cut solidbody, carved top, K-II on truss-rod cover

- **Body & Hardware:** double cutaway with rounded horns, carved maple top.
- **Neck:** K-II on truss-rod cover.
- **Pickups & Controls:** 2 humbucking pickups.

Les Paul SM (1980)

Single-cut solidbody, carved top, dot inlays, silver Sunburst finish

- **Body & Hardware:** contoured back, multiple-bound top, Silverburst finish.
- **Neck:** bound fingerboard, dot inlays, *SM* on truss-rod cover.
- **Pickups & Controls:** 2 humbucking pickups, 4 knobs, coil tap switch.

Les Paul Standard 82 (1980–82): Made in Kalamazoo plant, flamed maple top, uniform-depth binding in cutaway, 1-piece neck, *Standard 82* on truss-rod cover, nickel-plated hardware.

The Paul Deluxe (1980–85)

Thin single-cut solidbody, dot inlays, exposed-coil pickups

- **Body & Hardware:** thinsingle-cutaway solidbody, mahogany body, beveled edges around lower treble bout, no pickguard.
- **Neck:** unbound ebony fingerboard, dot inlays, some with *Firebrand* on truss-rod cover but not a Firebrand (branded logo) model.
- **Pickups & Controls:** 2 exposed-coil humbucking pickups, selector switch below tailpiece.

SG Artist (1981) / **SG-R1** (1980)

Double-cut solidbody, pointed horns, 2 switches, active electronics

- **Body & Hardware:** thicker body than standard SG, no pickguard.
- **Neck:** unbound ebony fingerboard, dot inlays, crown peghead inlay.
- **Pickups & Controls:** 2 humbucking pickups, active solid-state electronics, 4 knobs (2 numbered 0-5-0), 3-way toggle, 2-way toggle.

Sonex-180 (1980) / **Sonex-180 Deluxe** (1981–83)

Single-cut solidbody, bolt on neck, exposed-coil pickups

- **Body & Hardware:** Les Paul body size and shape, beveled edge on bass side, Multi-Phonic body (wood core, resin outer layer), Tune-o-matic bridge, pickguard covers three-quarters of body, chrome-plated hardware.
- **Neck:** bolt-on 3-piece maple neck, rosewood fingerboard, dot inlays, metal tuners, decal logo.
- **Pickups & Controls:** 2 exposed-coil Velvet Brick humbucking pickups, 3-way selector switch.

Sonex-180 Custom (1980–82): Coil-tap switch, ebony fingerboard.

335-S Deluxe (1980–82)

Thin double-cut solidbody, rounded horns (ES-335 shape)

- **Body & Hardware:** solid mahogany body, double rounded cutaways (like ES-335 but smaller), Tune-o-matic bridge, TP-6 tailpiece, triangular wing-shaped pickguard.
- **Neck:** bound ebony fingerboard, dot inlays, brass nut.
- **Pickups & Controls:** 2 Dirty Fingers exposed-coil humbucking pickups, coil-tap switch.

335-S Custom (1980): Unbound rosewood fingerboard, branded headstock logo (some routed for inlay but no inlay).

335-S Standard (1980): No coil tap, branded headstock logo (some routed for inlay but no inlay).

1981

ES-335 DOT (1981–90): Dot inlays stopbar tailpiece, gold-plated hardware optional with white finish.

Explorer I (1981–82)
See previous listing 1958.

Firebird II (1981–82)
Solidbody with treble horn longer than bass horn, 2 full-size humbuckers, TP-6 tailpiece

- **Body & Hardware:** reverse body shape, maple body with figured maple top cap, Tune-o-matic bridge, TP-6 fine-tune tailpiece, bound top, large backplate for electronics access, Antique Sunburst or Antique Fireburst finish.
- **Neck:** 3-piece maple neck, unbound rosewood fingerboard, dot inlays, pearl logo at tip of peghead.
- **Pickups & Controls:** 2 full-size humbucking pickups, active electronics 4 black barrel knobs, selector switch. 2 mini-switches for standard/active and brightness control.

Firebrand Les Paul (1981)
See previous entry for The Paul 1978.

Flying V I (1981–82)
See previous listing 1958.

Flying V FF 8 (1981): Made for Frankfurt (Germany) trade show, same specs as Flying V I.

Flying V Heritage (1981–82): Reissue of 1958 version, 3-piece Korina neck, Antique Natural, Ebony, Candy Apple Red, or white finish, serial number of letter followed by 3 digits (example: A 123).

Flying V CMT / The V (1981–85)
V-shaped solidbody, curly maple top
- **Body & Hardware:** maple body (earliest with mahogany body), curly maple top, no pickguard, bound top, vibrato optional, gold-plated hardware, Antique Sunburst, Antique Natural or Vintage Cherry Sunburst finish.
- **Neck:** maple, ebony fingerboard, dot inlays, pearl logo.
- **Pickups & Controls:** 2 Dirty Fingers humbucking pickups with exposed crème coils, 3 knobs in curving line, selector switch between upper knobs.

GGC-700 (1981–82)
Single-cut solidbody, flat top, oversized black pickguard
- **Body & Hardware:** single-cutaway solidbody, flat top, beveled edge on bass side, Tune-o-matic bridge, large black pickguard covers three-quarters of body, chrome-plated hardware.
- **Neck:** unbound rosewood fingerboard, dot inlays, decal logo *The Gibson Guitar Company*, metal keystone tuner buttons.
- **Pickups & Controls:** 2 humbucking pickups with exposed zebra coils, 4 black barrel knobs, selector switch near bridge, coil tap switch, jack into top.

L.P. XR-1 (1981–82)
Single-cut solidbody, 2 exposed-coil humbuckers, coil tap
- **Body & Hardware:** single cutaway, flat top, unbound top, Tobacco Sunburst, Cherry Sunburst or Goldburst finish.
- 3-piece maple neck, unbound rosewood fingerboard, dot inlay.
- 2 exposed-coil Dirty Fingers humbucking pickups, coil-tap switch.

L.P. XR-II (1981–82)
Single-cut solidbody, carved top, 2 covered humbuckers, coil tap
- **Body & Hardware:** flat or carved top of figured maple, laminated mahogany body, Nashville Tune-o-matic bridge, bound top, chrome-plated hardware, honey Sunburst or Vintage Cherry Sunburst finish
- **Neck:** 3-piece maple or 2-piece mahogany neck, unbound rosewood fingerboard, dot inlays, pearl logo, metal tuner buttons
- **Pickups & Controls:** 2 super humbucking pickups (some with metal-covered mini-humbuckers with no polepieces and *Gibson* embossed on pickup covers), coil-tap switch

RD Artist CMT (1981): Maple body, bound curly maple top, gold speed knobs, TP-6 fine-tune tailpiece, maple neck, 24¾-inch scale, bound ebony fingerboard, block inlays, chrome-plated hardware, Antique Cherry Sunburst or Antique Sunburst finish. Production: 100.

Sonex-180 Deluxe (1981–83)
See earlier entry for Sonix-180 1980.

Sonex Artist 1981–84: Active electronics, 2 standard humbuckers, 3 mini-switches (bright, compression, expansion), TP-6 tailpiece, no pickguard, *Artist* on truss-rod cover.

Victory MV-2 or MV-II (1981–84)
Double-cut solidbody, extended pointed horns, peghead points to bass side
- **Body & Hardware:** maple body, 13-inch wide,

asymmetrical double cutaway with extended horns, horns come to a point, wide-travel "Nashville" Tune-o-matic bridge, chrome-plated hardware, Candy Apple Red or Antique Fireburst finish.
- **Neck:** 3-piece bolt-on maple neck, bound rosewood fingerboard, dot inlay positioned near bass edge of fingerboard, 6-on-a-side tuner arrangement, peghead points to bass side, decal logo and *Victory* decal near nut.
- **Pickups & Controls:** velvet Brick zebra-coil neck pickup, special design black-coil humbucking bridge pickup, 2 knobs, coil-tap switch, 3-position slide switch.

Victory MV-10 or MV-X (1981–84): 2 zebra-coil humbucking pickups and 1 stacked-coil humbucking pickup (middle position), 2 knobs, master coil-tap switch, 5-position slide switch, bound ebony fingerboard, Antique Cherry Sunburst, Candy Apple Red or Twilight Blue finish.

1982

Chet Atkins CE (Standard) (1982–2005)
Single-cut solidbody classical, nylon strings
- **Body & Hardware:** 14½-inch wide, single cutaway, chambered mahogany back, spruce top (cedar optional (1994–95), simulated round soundhole, soundhole insert with signature and prewar script logo, rectangular bridge, multiple-bound top with brown outer layer, gold-plated hardware.
- **Neck:** 25½-inch scale, unbound rosewood fingerboard (ebony from 1996), 1.8-inch nut width (also specified as 1 $^{13}/_{16}$-inch and 1⅞-inch), slotted peghead, scalloped top edge of peghead, no logo (standard "dove wing" with logo from 1993).
- **Pickups & Controls:** transducer pickup, roller knobs recessed into upper bass side, individual trim pots accessible internally.

Chet Atkins CEC (1982–2005): Ebony fingerboard, 2-inch wide at nut.

Corvus I (1982–84)
Solidbody shaped like battle ax, six-on-a-side tuners, bolt-on neck
- **Body & Hardware:** solidbody with cutout along entire bass side of body, cutout on upper treble side, deep V-shaped cutout from bottom end almost to bridge, chrome-plated hardware, silver finish standard.
- **Neck:** bolt-on maple neck, 24¾-inch scale, unbound rosewood fingerboard, dot inlays, 6-on-a-side tuners, decal logo.
- **Pickups & Controls:** 1 humbucking pickup with black cover and no visible poles, pickup dipped in epoxy, 2 knobs, combination bridge/tailpiece with individual string adjustments.

Corvus II (1982–84): 2 pickups, 3 knobs.

Corvus III (1982–84): 3 high-output single-coil pickups, 2 knobs, 5-way switch.

Futura (1982–84)
Solidbody shaped like battle axe, six-on-a-side tuners, set neck
- **Body & Hardware:** neck-through-body, cutout along entire bass side of body, cutout on upper treble side, deep cutout from bottom end almost to bridge, Gibson/Kahler Supertone vibrato optional, large tailpiece with individually adjustable saddles, gold-plated hardware, Ebony, Ultra Violet or Pearl White finish.
- **Neck:** rosewood fingerboard, dot inlays, 6-on-a-side tuners.
- **Pickups & Controls:** 2 humbucking pickups with no visible poles, 2 knobs.

Guitar Trader Reissue (1982–c1985): Special order by Guitar Trader, a Gibson dealer in Redbank, New Jersey, serial number begins with 9, except for a few beginning with 0 (with thinner 1960-style neck). Production: less than 50.

'82

ES-369 (1982)
Thinbody double-cut archtop, narrow peghead, prewar script logo

- **Body & Hardware:** 16-inch semi-hollow archtop body of laminated maple, Tune-o-matic bridge, TP-6 tailpiece, single-ply cream-colored pickguard, single-bound top and back.
- **Neck:** single-bound rosewood fingerboard, pearloid trapezoid inlays, snakehead peghead, old-style script logo.
- **Pickups & Controls:** 2 Dirty Fingers pickups with exposed coils, 4 speed knobs, 1 selector switch, 1 mini-toggle coil-tap switch.

Explorer Korina (1982–84): Reissue of 1958 version, Korina body, Nashville wide-travel Tune-o-matic bridge, gold knobs, metal tuner buttons, standard 8-digit serial number, Candy Apple Red, Ebony, Ivory, or Antique Natural finish.

Les Paul Black Beauty '82 (1982–83): Multiply cream binding, unbound ebony fingerboard, trapezoid inlays, speed tuners, black finish, 4-digit serial number (some with additional standard 8-digit serial number).

Leo's Reissue (1982–c1985): Special order by Leo's Music, a Gibson dealer in Oakland, California, made in Nashville, inked-on serial number starts with letter *L* followed by a space.

Les Paul Silver Streak (1982)
Single-cut solidbody, carved top, silver finish

- **Body & Hardware:** single-cutaway solidbody, carved top, Tune-o-matic bridge, all silver finish.
- **Neck:** dot inlays Custom Shop decal on back of peghead, inked LE serial number and "reg." limited run number.
- **Pickups & Controls:** 2 humbucking pickups, 4 knobs, selector switch on upper bass bout.
Production: 1,000.

Les Paul 30th Anniversary (1982–83)
Single-cut solidbody, carved top, 30th Anniversary *at 19th fret*

- **Body & Hardware:** single-cutaway solidbody, carved maple top, mahogany back, Tune-o-matic bridge with spring retainer, uniform-depth binding in cutaway, all-gold finish.
- **Neck:** 3-piece mahogany neck, 1-piece neck optional, pearl trapezoid inlays, *30th Anniversary* engraved on inlay at 19th fret, nickel-plated hardware, serial number with A-, B- or C-prefix followed by 3 digits.
- **Pickups & Controls:** 2 PAF humbucking pickups, 4 knobs, selector switch on upper treble bout.

L.P. XR-III (1982): specs unavailable.

Moderne Heritage (1982–83)
Asymmetrical solidbody with V at bottom, wide flared headstock

- **Body & Hardware:** Korina solidbody with scooped treble side, Tune-o-matic bridge.
- **Neck:** unbound rosewood fingerboard, dot inlays, string guides on peghead, serial number of letter followed by 3 digits.
- **Pickups & Controls:** 2 humbucking pickups, 3 barrel knobs, gold-plated hardware.

Spirit I: (1982–87)
Double-cut solidbody, rounded horns, carved top, 1 humbucker

- **Body & Hardware:** combination bridge/tailpiece with individual string adjustments, tortoiseshell celluloid pickguard, chrome-plated hardware, silver finish standard.
- **Neck:** 3-piece maple neck, 24¾-inch scale, unbound rosewood fingerboard, 22 frets, dot inlays, plastic keystone tuner buttons, decal logo.
- **Pickups & Controls:** 1 exposed-coil humbucking pickup with crème coils, 2 barrel knobs.

Spirit II (1982–87): Curly maple top optional (1983), 2 pickups, 3 knobs, selector switch below knobs, no pickguard, bound top.

1983

ES-335 DOT CMT (1983–85): Custom Shop model, highly figured maple top and back, 2 PAF humbucking pickups, full-length maple centerblock, mahogany neck.

ES-357 (1983–84)
Thinbody double-cut archtop, 3 pickups, Mitch Holder model
- **Body & Hardware:** 16-inch semi-hollow body of laminated maple, 2-inch deep, curly maple top, no *f*-holes, TP-6 fine-tune tailpiece, single-bound top and back, Natural finish.
- **Neck:** 3-piece maple neck, bound ebony fingerboard, pearl block inlays, crown peghead inlay, bound peghead, gold-plated hardware.
- **Pickups & Controls:** 3 P-90 pickups with black soapbar covers or humbucking covers (polepieces across center), 4 knobs (3 volume, 1 master tone), selector switch, mini-toggle switch for middle pickup control.

Production: 7 from Kalamazoo Custom Shop (1983); a few more made in Nashville (1984).

Challenger I (1983–84)
Single-cut solidbody, bolt-on neck, standard peghead
- **Body & Hardware:** single-cutaway solidbody, flat top, pickguard surrounds pickup(s), combination bridge/tailpiece with individual string adjustments, chrome-plated hardware, silver finish standard.
- **Neck:** bolt-on maple neck, unbound rosewood fingerboard, dot inlays, standard peghead shape, decal logo.
- **Pickups & Controls:** 1 humbucking pickup with black cover and no visible poles, 2 knobs.

Challenger II (1983–84): 2 pickups, 3 knobs.

Explorer 83 (1983)
See earlier listing 1958.

Explorer Heritage (1983): Reissue of 1958 version, Korina body, black knobs, 3-piece Korina neck (first 8 with 1-piece neck), pearloid keystone tuner buttons, serial number of *1* followed by a space and 4 digits, Antique Natural, Ebony or Ivory finish. Production: 100.

Flying V Korina (1983): Same as Flying V Heritage except for black barrel knobs, 8-digit serial number.

Flying V 83 (1983)
See earlier listing 1958.

Invader (1983–88, prototypes from 1980)
Single-cut solidbody, bolt-on neck, stopbar tailpiece
- **Body & Hardware:** single-cutaway mahogany solidbody, beveled bass-side edge, Tune-o-matic bridge, stop tailpiece, chrome-plated hardware.
- **Neck:** bolt-on maple neck, ebony fingerboard, dot inlays, standard Gibson peghead shape, decal logo.
- **Pickups & Controls:** 2 ceramic magnet humbucking pickups with exposed zebra coils, 4 knobs, 3-way selector switch.

Invader variations (designed to use up bodies, model names unknown) (1988–89):
- 1 narrow pickup, 2 knobs, Kahler vibrato, set maple neck, ebony fingerboard, dot inlays, crown peghead inlay, black chrome hardware.
- 2 humbucking pickups with black plastic covers and no visible polepieces, 2 knobs, 1 switch, Kahler Flyer vibrato, pearloid pickguard covers most of treble side of body, jack into pickguard, set neck, unbound ebony fingerboard, dot inlays, Explorer-style peghead with 6-on-a-side tuner arrangement, black chrome hardware.

Les Paul Reissue (1983–1991) / **Les Paul '59 Flametop Reissue** (1991–current) / **Les Paul '60 Flametop Reissue** (1991–current)
Copy of 1958–60 Les Paul Standard, single-cut solidbody, carved top, trapezoid inlays, inked serial number

'83

- **Body & Hardware:** highly flamed maple top (plain-top, quilt top or killer top from 1999), binding inside cutaway same depth as other top binding, nickel-plated hardware, Cherry Sunburst finish, Custom Authentic aging treatment optional from 2001, Vintage Original Spec aging treatment optional from 2006.
- **Neck:** standard-production neck (optional fat '59 or slim '60 neck profile 1991–current), inked-on 1950s-style serial number with 1st digit corresponding to last digit of year (earliest with 9 as 1st digit, standard 8-digit serial number in control cavity; R9 or R0 in control cavity from 1993), no model name on truss-rod cover.
- **Pickups & Controls:** 2 humbucking pickups, 4 knobs, selector switch on upper bass bout.

Les Paul Reissue Gold-top (1983–91): Gold-top finish, humbucking pickups (stacked-coil P-100s with soapbar covers from 1990).

Les Paul Spotlight Special (1983–84)
Single-cut solidbody, carved top with dark center piece
- **Body & Hardware:** 3-piece carved top with curly maple outer pieces and walnut center, multiple cream-brown-cream top binding, gold-plated hardware, Antique Natural finish.
- **Neck:** bound rosewood fingerboard, trapezoid inlays, walnut peghead veneer, oval pearloid tuner buttons, serial number of 83 followed by a space and 4-digit ranking.
- **Pickups & Controls:** 2 PAF humbucking pickups, 4 knobs, selector switch on upper bass bout.
Production: at least 211.

Les Paul Standard 83 (1983): Highly figured maple top, PAF-reissue humbucking pickups, Tune-o-matic bridge, 1-piece mahogany neck, rosewood fingerboard, pearl trapezoid inlays, nickel-plated hardware, Antique Natural, Vintage Cherry Sunburst or Vintage Sunburst finish.

Les Paul Standard Special (1983): 2 PAF humbucking pickups, cream binding, bound ebony fingerboard, pearl trapezoid inlays, metal keystone tuner buttons, gold-plated hardware, Cardinal Red finish.

Les Paul Studio (1983–current)
Single-cut solidbody, carved top, no binding
- **Body & Hardware:** single cutaway, mahogany back, carved maple top, Tune-o-matic bridge, black pickguard, no binding anywhere, chrome- or gold-plated hardware.
- **Neck:** maple neck (mahogany from 1990), rosewood or ebony fingerboard, dot inlay (trapezoid from 1990, ¾-scale 1999–2000, full-size from 2001, no inlays with platinum finish), pearloid keystone tuner buttons, *Studio* on truss-rod cover, *Les Paul Model* decal on peghead, decal logo, plastic keystone tuner buttons.
- **Pickups & Controls:** 2 PAF humbucking pickups with covers, 4 knobs, selector switch on upper bass bout.

Map-shape (1983)
Body shaped like United States
- **Body & Hardware:** mahogany body shaped like United States, combination bridge/tailpiece with individual string adjustments, Natural Mahogany finish standard, 9 made with American flag finish.
- **Neck:** 3-piece maple neck, ebony fingerboard, dot inlays crown peghead inlay, pearl logo, metal tuner buttons.
- **Pickups & Controls:** 2 humbucking pickups, 4 knobs, 1 switch.
Production: Promotional model for dealers only.

Special I (1983–85)
Double-cut solidbody, pointed horns, 1 humbucker
- **Body & Hardware:** solid mahogany double-cutaway body, pointed horns, combination bridge/tailpiece with individual string adjustments.
- **Neck:** unbound rosewood fingerboard, dot inlays, *Special* on truss-rod cover.

- **Pickups & Electronics:** 1 exposed-coil humbucking pickup, 2 knobs, jack into top.

Special II (1983–85): 2 exposed-coil humbucking pickups.

1984

Black Knight Custom (1984)
Single-cut solidbody, bolt-on neck, 6-on-a-side tuners
- **Body & Hardware:** single-cutaway solidbody, flat top with beveled edges, 4 knobs, 3-way selector switch near knobs, Kahler vibrato, black chrome-plated hardware, Ebony finish
- **Neck:** bolt-on neck, rosewood fingerboard, dot inlays, 6-on-a-side tuner arrangement,
- **Pickups & Controls:** 2 humbucking pickups.

Explorer (1984–89)
See earlier listing 1958.

Explorer III (1984–85)
Angular solidbody, 3 pickups
- **Body & Hardware:** alder body, Tune-o-matic bridge, locking nut vibrato system optional, Alpine White or military-style camouflage finish.
- **Neck:** maple, unbound rosewood fingerboard, dot inlays, metal tuners, decal logo.
- **Pickups & Controls:** 3 soapbar HP-90 pickups, 2 knobs, 2 selector switches.

Flying V XPL (1984–86) Kahler vibrato or combination bridge/tailpiece with individual string adjustments (Tune-o-matic optional from 1985), maple neck, unbound ebony fingerboard, Explorer-style peghead, 6-on-a-side tuner arrangement.

Les Paul Super Custom (1984): Prototypes for Steve Perry model, earliest made in Kalamazoo factory, then in Nashville, 1 humbucking pickup with cover, 1 exposed-coil humbucking pickup, curly maple top, back and sides covered with curly maple veneer, multiple-bound top, 3-piece maple neck, single-bound fingerboard, Super 400-style slashed-block inlays, *LE* on truss-rod cover, Cherry Sunburst finish all over.

Les Paul Double-Cutaway XPL (1984–86):
Double-cut solidbody, carved top, 6-on-a-side tuners
- **Body & Hardware:** symmetrical double-cutaway, carved top, Gibson/Kahler Supertone vibrato or Tune-o-matic bridge, bound top, 24¾-inch scale, chrome-plated hardware.
- **Neck:** bound ebony fingerboard, 22 frets, dot inlays, 6-on-a-side tuner configuration, peghead points to treble side, decal logo.
- **Pickups & Controls:** 2 humbucking pickups, 4 knobs, selector switch above knobs.

Les Paul Double-Cutaway XPL/400 (1984): 400-series electronics, 1 Dirty Fingers humbucking pickup and 2 single-coil pickups, master tone and master volume knob, 3 mini-switches for on/off pickup control, push/pull volume control for coil tap, rosewood or ebony fingerboard, cream binding.

Les Paul Studio Custom (1984–85): Multiple-bound top, bound rosewood fingerboard, gold-plated hardware.

Les Paul Studio Standard (1984–87): Cream binding on top, cream-bound rosewood fingerboard.

Les Paul XPL (1984)
Thin single-cut solidbody, carved top, 6-on-a-side tuners
- **Body & Hardware:** single-cutaway solidbody, mahogany back, carved maple top.
- **Neck:** Explorer peghead, 6-on-a-side tuner configuration.
- **Pickups & Controls:** 2 humbucking pickups.

Super 400C 50th Anniversary (1984): BJB floating pickup, engraved heelcap, binding on back of

peghead comes to point (similar to Citation binding but with no volute), *Super 400 1935 50th Anniversary 1984* engraved in abalone inlay on back of peghead, Kluson Sealfast tuners with pearl buttons.

1985

Explorer Black Hardware (1985): Kahler vibrato standard, black hardware.

Explorer 400/400+ (1985–86): 400-series electronics, 1 Dirty Fingers humbucking pickup and 2 single-coil pickups, master tone and master volume knob, 3 mini-switches for on/off pickup control, push/pull volume control for coil tap, Kahler Flyer vibrato, black chrome hardware, Alpine White, Ebony, Ferrari Red or Pewter finish.

Explorer Synthesizer (1985): Roland 700 synthesizer system, Alpine White or Ebony finish.

Explorer III Black Hardware (1985): Kahler vibrato standard, black hardware.

EXP 425 (1985–86)
Angular solidbody, humbucker and 2 single-coils
- **Body & Hardware:** angular solid mahogany body, no pickguard, black hardware, Kahler vibrato.
- **Neck:** ebony fingerboard, six-on-a-side tuner arrangement.
- **Pickups & Controls:** 1 humbucking and 2 single-coil pickups, no pickup covers, 2 knobs, 3 mini-toggle switches.

Flying V 400/400+ (1985–86): 400-series electronics, 1 Dirty Fingers humbucking pickup and 2 single-coil pickups, master tone and master volume knob, 3 mini-switches for on/off pickup control, push/pull volume control for coil tap, Kahler Flyer vibrato, black chrome hardware, Alpine White, Ebony, Ferrari Red or Pewter finish.

Flying V Black Hardware (1985): Kahler vibrato standard, black hardware.

Flying V XPL Black Hardware (1985): Black hardware, Kahler vibrola standard, Ebony, Alpine White, or red finish.

Les Paul Special 400 (1985): 400-series electronics, 1 Dirty Fingers humbucking pickup and 2 single-coil pickups, master tone and master volume knob, 3 mini-switches for on/off pickup control, push/pull volume control for coil tap, vibrato, early with rosewood fingerboard, later with ebony.

Les Paul Studio Synthesizer (1985): Roland 700 synthesizer system.

Q-100 (Alpha Series) (1985)
Double-cut asymmetrical solidbody, bolt-on neck
- **Body & Hardware:** double-cutaway body shape similar to Victory MV, Tune-o-matic bridge, optional Kahler Flyer vibrato, chrome-plated hardware without Kahler, black chrome hardware with Kahler, Ebony or Panther Pink finish.
- **Neck:** bolt-on neck, ebony fingerboard, dot inlays, 6-on-a-side tuner arrangement.
- **Pickups & Controls:** 1 Dirty Fingers humbucking pickup.

Q-200 (1985): 1 HP-90 single-coil pickup in neck position, 1 Dirty Fingers humbucking pickup in bridge position, coil tap, Kahler Flyer vibrato, Ebony, Alpine White, Ferrari Red or Panther Pink finish.

Q-300/Q-3000 (1985): 3 HP-90 single-coil pickups, 2 knobs, selector switch, "mid" switch, Kahler Flyer vibrato, Ebony or red finish.

Q-4000 (1985) / **400** (1986): 1 humbucking pickup, 1 Dirty Fingers humbucking pickup and 2 single-coil pickups, master tone and master volume knob, 3 mini-switches for on/off pickup control, push/pull volume control for coil tap, Kahler Flyer vibrato, earliest with neck-through-body, Ebony, Ferrari Red or Panther Pink finish.

SG 400 (1985–86)

Double-cut solidbody, pointed horns, 3 pickups, 3 mini-switches

- **Body & Hardware:** solid mahogany double-cutaway body, pointed horns, vibrato, black hardware.
- **Neck:** bound rosewood fingerboard, dot inlays.
- **Pickups & Controls:** 400-series electronics, 1 Dirty Fingers humbucking pickup, 2 single-coil pickups, master tone and master volume knob, 3 mini-switches for on/off pickup control, push/pull volume control for coil tap.

Spirit I XPL (1985–86): 1 pickup with crème coils, Kahler Flyer vibrato, bound top, bound fingerboard, Explorer-style peghead with 6-on-a-side tuner arrangement.

Spirit II XPL (1985–86): 2 pickups, 3 knobs, selector switch below knobs, bound top, bound fingerboard, Explorer-style peghead with 6-on-a-side tuner arrangement.

XPL Custom (1985–86)

Angular solidbody, cutout in lower treble horn

- **Body & Hardware:** solidbody somewhat similar to Explorer but with sharply pointed horns, cutout at lower treble horn, bound curly maple top, locking nut vibrato system, bound top, Cherry Sunburst or Alpine White finish.
- **Neck:** dot inlays 6-on-a-side tuner configuration.
- **Pickups & Controls:** 2 Dirty Fingers exposed-coil humbucking pickups, 2 knobs, 1 switch.

XPL Standard (1985)

Solidbody with shape similar to small Firebird, 2 exposed-coil humbuckers

- **Body & Hardware:** solidbody, "sculptured" edges, small Firebird shape, Tune-o-matic bridge or Kahler Flyer vibrato, chrome-plated or black chrome hardware, Ebony, Kerry Green or Alpine White finish.
- **Neck:** 6-on-a-side tuner configuration.

- **Pickups & Controls:** 2 Dirty Fingers exposed-coil humbucking pickups.

1986

Chet Atkins CGP (1986–87)

Asymmetrical solidbody, 2 mini toggles, bolt-on neck

- **Body & Hardware:** contoured mahogany body, flat-mount bridge/tailpiece with individual string adjustments, Kahler Flyer vibrato optional, gold-plated hardware, Wine Red finish.
- **Neck:** bolt-on maple neck, ebony fingerboard, 25½-inch scale.
- **Pickups & Controls:** 2 single-coil pickups tapped for normal and high output, 2 knobs (volume and tone), 2 mini-toggles for ohm tap, 3-way selector switch.

Production: Catalogued but few if any produced.

Chet Atkins Country Gentleman (1986–2005)

Thin single-cut archtop, red rectangular inlays

- **Body & Hardware:** 17-inch wide, rounded cutaway, thinline semi-hollowbody, Tune-o-matic bridge, ebony bridge base with pearl inlay, Bigsby vibrato with curved tubular arm (optional from 1993), 7-ply top binding, 5-ply back binding, bound *f*-holes.
- **Neck:** laminated maple neck, 25½-inch scale, 21 frets, unbound ebony fingerboard, red rectangular inlays positioned on bass edge of fingerboard, 1¾-inch nut width, unbound peghead, crown peghead inlay, metal tuner buttons.
- **Pickups & Controls:** 2 humbucking pickups, 3 knobs (2 volume, 1 master tone) and 3-way selector switch on lower treble bout, master volume knob on cutaway bout.

ES-335 Studio (1986–91), **ES-Studio** (1991): No *f*-holes, 2 Dirty Fingers humbucking pickups with covers (earliest with exposed-coil PAF humbuckers, mahogany neck, unbound rosewood fingerboard

(earliest with ebony), dot inlays, no peghead ornament, decal logo, Ebony or Cherry finish.

Les Paul CMT (1986–mid 1989)
Single-cut solidbody, carved top, curly top, metal jackplate, made primarily for Sam Ash stores
- **Body & Hardware:** single-cutaway solidbody, carved curly maple top, deeper binding inside cutaway than other top binding.
- **Neck:** bound rosewood fingerboard, trapezoid inlays, Les Paul signature and *MODEL* silkscreened on peghead, stamped 8-digit serial number.
- **Pickups & Controls:** 2 humbucking pickups, 4 knobs, selector switch on upper bass bout, metal jack plate.

SG Reissue (1986–87) / SG '62 Reissue (1988–90) / Les Paul SG '61 Reissue (1993–97) / SG '61 Reissue (1998–current) (also see Les Paul/SG Standard Reissue)
Double-cut solidbody, pointed horns, trapezoid inlays
- **Body & Hardware:** double-cutaway solid mahogany body, pointed horns, Tune-o-matic bridge, small pickguard, nickel-plated hardware, Heritage Cherry finish.
- **Neck:** bound rosewood fingerboard, trapezoid inlays, crown peghead inlay, plastic keystone tuner buttons.
- **Pickups & Controls:** 2 humbucking pickups, 4 knobs, selector switch near pickguard, jack in top.

US-1: (1986–90)
Double-cut solidbody, Strat-like shape, split-diamond inlays
- **Body & Hardware:** double cutaway solidbody similar to Fender Stratocaster, maple top, mahogany back, Chromyte (balsa) core, Tune-o-matic bridge or Kahler locking nut vibrato system, bound top and back, gold-plated hardware with Tune-o-matic bridge, black chrome hardware with Kahler vibrato.
- **Neck:** maple, 25½-inch scale, bound ebony

fingerboard, split-diamond inlays, bound peghead, 6-on-a-side tuner arrangement, large raised plastic logo (pearl from 1987), mini-Grover tuners.
- **Pickups & Controls:** 3 humbucking pickups (2 with stacked-coil design) with no visible poles, 3 mini-switches for on/off pickup control, 2 knobs (push/pull volume control for coil tap).

1987

Chet Atkins Phasar (1987)
Double-cut asymmetrical solidbody, 2 narrow humbuckers
- **Body & Hardware:** asymmetrical double cutaway solidbody.
- **Neck:** rosewood fingerboard, 25½-inch scale, dot inlays, 6-on-a-side tuner arrangement.
- **Pickups & Controls:** 2 narrow humbucking pickups with no visible poles, 2 knobs.
Production: 6 (3 with vibrato, 3 without).

Chet Atkins SST (1987–2005)
Single-cut solidbody acoustic, steel strings, Chet Atkins signature on body
- **Body & Hardware:** single cutaway, spruce top, mahogany body with Chromyte (balsa) center, simulated round soundhole, soundhole insert with signature and prewar script logo (no soundhole from 1993, signature decal near fingerboard from 1993), rectangular ebony bridge (belly bridge from 1993), bound top, gold-plated hardware, Antique Natural, Alpine White or Ebony finish.
- **Neck:** mahogany, 21 frets, 25½-inch scale, unbound ebony fingerboard, dot inlay (star inlay from 1993), 1¹¹⁄₁₆-inch nut width, solid peghead, scalloped top edge of peghead (standard "dove wing" peghead from 1991), no peghead logo or ornament (prewar-style script logo from 1991, star inlay from 1993).
- **Pickups & Controls:** transducer bridge pickup with built-in preamp, 2 knobs on top (knobs on rim from 1993).

A BRIGHT NEW ERA

Following the rapid decline of the company in the final years of Norlin's ownership, and the closure of the Kalamazoo plant in 1984, Gibson was sold to former Harvard Business School classmates Henry Juskiewicz, David Berryman, and Gary Zebrowski in January 1986 for $5 million. After the virtually inevitable teething troubles that new regimes are bound to experience, and the cool reception given to a raft of non-Gibsony new models, Gibson's new leaders began steadily reclaiming the brand. Much of the return to strength came in recognizing the appeal of the classic models of the 1950s and early '60s, and in providing appropriately accurate reissues of these – a trend that was foreshadowed by the success of the Heritage Series of the early 1980s, and further confirmed by the Historic Collection in the early 1990s (Fender, meanwhile, was following much the same reissue-paved road back to liquidity in its post-CBS years). Saved from what most analysts agree was the brink of extinction by three businessmen who, for a change, showed a keen interest in guitars, Gibson was not only out of the woods, but on the way to becoming the biggest and strongest company it had ever been.

A raft of well-targeted new models also no doubt helped to get Gibsons back into the hands of players again. On one side of the coin, guitars such as the well-received SG Reissue of 1986 addressed guitarists' continuing desires for the great Gibsons of days gone by, while new variations on old themes – such as the ES-335 Studio, Les Paul Studio Lite, Les Paul Custom Lite, Explorer 90 and Flying V 90 – updated the legends to suit contemporary playing needs.

1987

Les Paul Custom Lite (1987–89)

Thin single-cut solidbody, carved top, block inlays, 3 knobs

- **Body & Hardware:** 1⅝-inch deep (⅜-inch thinner than Les Paul Custom), contoured back, Floyd Rose vibrato or Tune-o-matic bridge and stopbar tailpiece, chrome- or gold-plated hardware (black chrome 1989).
- **Neck:** ebony fingerboard, block inlay.
- **Pickups & Controls:** 2 PAF humbucking pickups (SW-5 sidewinder pickup in neck position, L-8 humbucking pickup in bridge position, black pickup covers with no visible poles, 1989), 2 volume knobs, master tone knob, coil-tap switch, pickup selector switch on upper bass bout.

Les Paul Jr Double Cutaway (1987–92, 1995): Double cutaway with rounded horns, P-90 pickup with black "dog-ear" cover (200 with P-100 stacked-coil humbucker, 1990–92), Tune-o-matic bridge, metal tuner buttons (plastic from 1989), chrome-

plated hardware (nickel 1990–92).

Les Paul Studio Lite (1987–98)

Thin single-cut solidbody, carved top, pearl logo

- **Body & Hardware:** 1⅝-inch deep solidbody, carved top, contoured back, Tune-o-matic bridge, stop tailpiece (Floyd Rose vibrato optional 1989), chrome plated hardware (gold or black with various finishes).
- **Neck:** unbound ebony fingerboard, dot inlay (trapezoid from 1991), *Les Paul Model* peghead decal, pearl logo, plain truss-rod cover.
- 2 humbucker pickups (black covers 1989, exposed coils 1991), 2 knobs, coil-tap switch.

SG Les Paul Custom (1987–90)

See earlier listing.

SG Elite (1987–89)

Double-cut solidbody, pointed horns, block inlays, locking nut

- **Body & Hardware:** solid mahogany double-cutaway body, pointed horns, Tune-o-matic bridge, TP-6 fine-tune tailpiece, gold-plated hardware, Pearl White or Metallic Sunset finish.
- **Neck:** bound ebony fingerboard, block inlays, locking nut, crown peghead inlay.
- **Pickups & Controls:** 2 Spotlight humbucking pickups, coil-tap switch.

SR-71 (1987–89)
Double-cut solidbody, Strat-like shape, set neck, designed by Wayne Charvel
- **Body & Hardware:** shape similar to Fender Stratocaster, Ebony, Nuclear Yellow or Alpine White finish. Floyd Rose locking nut vibrato system.
- **Neck:** glued-in maple neck, 25½-inch scale, 6-on-a-side tuner arrangement, point on treble side of peghead, prewar script logo, Custom Shop model, 250 made, limited edition number on truss-rod cover.
- **Pickups & Controls:** 1 humbucking and 2 single-coil pickups.
Production: 250.

U-2 / Mach II (1987–90)
Double-cut solidbody, Strat-like shape, raised plastic peghead logo
- **Body & Hardware:** asymmetrical double-cutaway solidbody similar to Fender Stratocaster, basswood body, contoured back, bound top. Floyd Rose vibrato, black chrome hardware.
- **Neck:** maple neck, 25½-inch scale, unbound rosewood fingerboard, 24 frets, dot inlays, unbound peghead, 6-on-a-side tuner arrangement, large raised plastic logo.
- **Pickups & Controls:** 2 single-coil pickups and 1 HPAF humbucking pickup, 2 Spotlight humbucking pickups optional, 2 knobs, 3 mini switches.

WRC (1987–89)
Double-cut solidbody, Strat-like shape, 3 mini switches, designed by Wayne Charvel
- **Body & Hardware:** alder body similar to Fender Stratocaster, beveled lower bass bout, Floyd Rose or Kahler vibrato, Ebony, Honeyburst or Ferrari Red finish.
- **Neck:** bolt-on maple neck, 25½-inch scale, ebony fingerboard, dot inlays, 6-on-a-side tuner arrangement, point on treble side of peghead, *WRC* or *WC* on truss-rod cover, prewar script logo (earliest with Charvel decal on peghead).
- **Pickups & Controls:** 1 humbucking pickup and 2 stacked-coil humbucking pickups with black covers and no polepieces, 3 on/off mini-switches, push/pull volume control for coil tap.

1988

Chet Atkins CE Showcase Edition (July 1988 guitar of the month): Vintage Sunburst finish. Production: 200 for US distribution, 50 for overseas.

ES-335 Showcase Edition (Apr. 1988 guitar of the month): EMG pickups, beige finish. Production: 200 for US distribution, 50 for overseas.

Explorer 90 (1988)
Angular solidbody, strings through body
- **Body & Hardware:** angular mahogany solidbody, Tune-o-matic bridge, lightning-bolt tailpiece with strings through body, Floyd Rose vibrato optional, black chrome hardware, Alpine White, Ebony or Luna Silver finish.
- **Neck:** 25½-inch scale, ebony fingerboard, split-diamond inlays, pearl logo.
- **Pickups & Controls:** 1 humbucking pickup, 2 knobs.

Flying V 90 (1988)
V-shaped solidbody, split-diamond inlays
- **Body & Hardware:** Floyd Rose vibrato optional, black chrome hardware, Alpine White, Ebony or Nuclear Yellow finish.

B.B. ONBOARD, CHET ON THE G-RUN

Nothing helps to get a guitar-maker back on track like a few good artist endorsements, and Gibson's new owners had the job of reviving the legendary brand made just that little bit easier with help from the strong shoulders of a handful of very prominent players. After years of unsolicited Gibson promotion for the ES-355 and related models, B.B. King had officially signed on with the company with the release of the B.B. King Standard and B.B. King Custom in 1980 (renamed Lucille Standard and Lucille respectively in 1981). Although King's endorsement arrived right alongside Gibson's darkest hour under Norlin, having his models at the head of the ES line no doubt helped to give some credence to the brand through its transitional phase in the mid 1980s.

Chet Atkins's legacy as an electric guitar endorsee, and to some extent designer, runs roughly parallel to that of Les Paul's. Both had input on the design of some of the most formative and successful electric models of the 1950s – Atkins with Gretsch, Paul with Gibson – and each continued to influence the evolution of the guitars that carried their names on and off through the following decades. Having severed his association with Gretsch in 1978, Atkins turned to Gibson in the early 1980s, mainly in an effort to find a company that would develop his idea for a nylon guitar string with a steel core that could react with a magnetic pickup (Atkins saw nylon-string guitars as a means of easing his affliction with brittle fingernails, which were continually chipping when used to pluck steel-string guitars). Gibson took up the idea and ran with it, and the revolutionary Chet Atkins CEC (Cutaway Electric Classical) of 1982 was the result. In 1986 an entire Chet Atkins line was released, which included the Chet Atkins Country Gentleman (formerly a leading model for Gretsch) and Chet Atkins CGP, and in 1987 the Chet Atkins Phasar and SST – the latter the steel-stringed equivalent of the CEC. Still further variations on these themes and others followed in the coming years.

- **Neck:** 25½-inch scale, unbound ebony fingerboard, split-diamond inlays, pearl logo.
- **Pickups & Controls:** 1 humbucking pickup.

Howard Roberts Fusion II (1988–90): See earlier listing 1979.

Junior Pro (1988)
Single-cut solidbody, flat top, humbucker with black cover, no Les Paul designation
- **Body & Hardware:** single cutaway mahogany body, (beveled waist on treble side, small pickguard extends from treble-side waist to end of fingerboard, Steinberger KB-X locking-nut vibrato, black chrome hardware.
- **Neck:** ebony fingerboard, dot inlays, decal logo.
- **Pickups & Controls:** slim-coil humbucking pickup

with black cover and no visible polepieces, 2 knobs.

Les Paul Custom Showcase Edition (Mar. 1988 guitar of the month): EMG pickups, Ruby finish. Production: 200 for US distribution, 50 for overseas.

Les Paul Custom Lite Showcase Edition (Aug. 1988 guitar of the month): EMG pickups, active electronics, gold-top finish. Production: 200 for US distribution, 50 for overseas.

Les Paul Pro Showcase Edition (Dec. 1988 guitar of the month): Gold-top finish. Production: 200 for US distribution, 50 for overseas.

Les Paul Jr Double Cutaway Special (1988):

Double cutaway with rounded horns, Tune-o-matic bridge, selector switch on treble side near bridge, chrome-plated hardware, metal tuner buttons, *Les Paul Model* on peghead, metal tuner buttons.

Les Paul Standard Showcase Edition (June 1988): EMG pickups, Silverburst finish. Production: 200 for US distribution, 50 for overseas.

SG Custom Showcase Edition (October 1988): EMG pickups, Ferrari Red finish. Production: 200 for US distribution, 50 for overseas.

SG '62 Reissue (1988–90)
See earlier listing 1963 for specs.

SG '62 Showcase Edition (April 1988 guitar of the month): EMG pickups, blue finish. Production: 200 for US distribution, 50 for overseas.

SG 90 Single (1988–90)
Double-cut solidbody, pointed horns, strings through body
- **Body & Hardware:** pearloid pickguard, strings mounted through body, Floyd Rose vibrato optional, Alpine White, Metallic Turquoise, or Heritage Cherry finish.
- **Neck:** unbound ebony fingerboard, 25½-inch scale, 2-piece split-diamond inlay, crown peghead inlay, pearl logo.
- **Pickups & Controls:** 1 humbucking pickup with black cover.

SG 90 Double (1988–90): 1 oblong single-coil pickup mounted diagonally in neck position, 1 black-covered humbucking pickup in bridge position, 2 knobs, push/pull for coil tap, selector switch between knobs.

U-2 Showcase Edition (Nov. 1988 guitar of the month): EMG pickups. Production: 200 for US distribution, 50 for overseas.

WRC Showcase Edition (Sept. 1988 guitar of the month): 3 EMG pickups (1 humbucking, 2 single-coil), 3 knobs, 4 toggle switches, Kahler vibrato, Sperzel tuners. Production: 200 for US distribution, 50 for overseas.

1989-90

Chet Atkins (JS) Double (1989–91): See Johnny Smith Double 1963.

Chet Atkins SST 12-string (1990–94): Star fingerboard inlay, scalloped top edge of peghead, prewar script logo, gold-plated hardware, Antique Natural, Alpine White, Wine Red or Ebony finish.

Chet Atkins Tennessean (1990–2005)
Thinbody single-cut archtop, dot inlays, near edge of fingerboard
- **Body & Hardware:** 16½-inch wide, 1⅝-inch deep, single rounded cutaway, laminated maple back and sides with Chromyte (balsa) center block, Tune-o-matic bridge, stopbar tailpiece, clear pickguard with silver paint on back and model name stenciled in black, single-bound top and back.
- **Neck:** unbound ebony fingerboard, 25½-inch scale, dot inlay positioned closer to bass edge of fingerboard, 1¾-inch nut width, clear plastic truss-rod cover back-painted silver, Chet Atkins signature peghead decal, plastic tuner buttons.
- **Pickups & Controls:** 2 humbucking pickups.

ES-175D CMT (1989–90): Curly maple top, bound ebony fingerboard, bound peghead, gold-plated hardware.

ES-335 Reissue (1990–current): Dot inlay (some limited runs with black binding, ebony fingerboard, small block inlays, 1998–99), stopbar tailpiece.

ES-775 Classic Beauty (1990–93)

Single-cut archtop, pointed horn, slotted-block inlay

- **Body & Hardware:** body & Hardware:16½-inch wide, figured laminated maple body, pointed cutaway, gold-plated hardware.
- **Neck:** 3-ply maple neck, bound ebony fingerboard, slotted-block inlay.
- **Pickups & Controls:** 2 humbucking pickups, 4 knobs, selector switch.

Explorer 90 Double (1989–90): Single-coil neck pickup, humbucking bridge pickup, 2 knobs, push/pull volume knob for coil tap, selector switch between knobs.

Flying V 90 Double (1989–90) 1 single-coil and 1 double-coil pickup, 2 knobs, push/pull volume knob for coil tap, Tune-o-matic bridge, Floyd Rose vibrato optional, pearl logo, Alpine White, Ebony or Luna Silver finish.

Les Paul Custom 35th Anniversary (1989): 3 humbucking pickups, *35th Anniversary* etched on middle peghead inlay, 1959-style inked-on serial number.

Les Paul Junior II (1989): Single cutaway, tune-o-matic bridge, 2 black soapbar P-100 pickups, *Les Paul Special* on peghead.

Les Paul Standard P-100 (1989): P-100 stacked humbucking pickups with soapbar covers, gold-top finish.

Les Paul Classic (1990–current)
Single-cut solidbody, carved top, no pickup covers, inked serial number
- **Body & Hardware:** single-cutaway solidbody, carved maple top, uniform-depth binding inside cutaway, *1960* on pickguard (some without pickguard), nickel-plated hardware.
- **Neck:** low-profile neck, *Les Paul Model* on peghead *Classic* on truss-rod cover (*Les Paul Classic* silkscreen from 1993), 1960 style serial

number with 1st digit corresponding to last digit of year.
- **Pickups & Controls:** 2 exposed-coil humbucking pickups, 4 knobs, selector switch on upper bass bout.

1991

Chet Atkins SST Celebrity Series (1991–93): Gold-plated hardware, Ebony finish.

Chet Atkins Studio Classic (1991–93)
Single-cut solidbody acoustic, fleur de lis on peghead
- **Body & Hardware:** single cutaway, hollow mahogany back, fan-braced spruce top, controls on rim, no soundhole, flared bridge ends, abalone top border, cocobolo wood bindings, top inlaid at end of fingerboard with rosewood and abalone fleur-de-lis (no top inlay, 1993), gold-plated hardware, Antique Natural finish.
- **Neck:** 26-inch scale, V-end ebony fingerboard (asymmetrical with treble-side extension, 1993), 2-inch nut width, small *CGP* inlay at 7th fret, no other fingerboard inlay, slotted peghead, peghead narrows toward top, rosewood peghead veneer, prewar style *The Gibson* logo in pearl (postwar logo, 1993), small fleur-de-lis peghead inlay.
- **Pickups & Controls:** under-saddle pickup, controls on rim.

ES-135 2nd version (1991–2003)
Thinbody single-cut archtop, pointed horn, dot inlays
- **Body & Hardware:** 16-inch laminated maple/poplar/maple semi-hollowbody, 2¼-inch deep, pointed cutaway, *f*-holes (no *f*-holes from 2002), Tune-o-matic bridge, trapeze tailpiece (stopbar from 2002), chrome-plated hardware (some gold-plated, 1998–99).
- **Neck:** maple, unbound rosewood fingerboard, dot inlays, model name decal on peghead, decal logo.

- **Pickups & Controls:** 2 P-100 stacked-coil humbucking pickups (humbuckers optional, 1998–2002, standard from 2003), 4 knobs, selector switch on upper bass bout.

ES-175 Reissue (1991–2005): See earlier listing 1949.

ES-335 Reissue (1991–98): See earlier listing 1958.

Explorer '76 (1991–2003): See earlier listing 1976.

Firebird V (1991–current): See earlier listing 1958.

Firebird V Celebrity Series (1991–93): Reverse body, black finish, white pickguard, gold-plated hardware.

Flying V '67 (1991–2003): See earlier listing 1958.

Herb Ellis Signature ES-165 (1991–2004)
Single-cut archtop, pointed horn, 1 humbucker
- **Body & Hardware:** 16-inch full-depth archtop, pointed cutaway, Tune-o-matic bridge on rosewood base, T-shaped tailpiece with zigzag wires, multiply top binding, single-bound back, gold-plated hardware.
- **Neck:** mahogany neck, bound rosewood fingerboard, double-parallelogram inlay, decal model name and logo on peghead (crown peghead inlay, pearl logo from 2002).
- **Pickups & Controls:** 1 humbucking pickup, 2 knobs (1 floating mini-humbucking pickup, control knob in pickguard from 2002).

Howard Roberts Fusion III (1991–current): See earlier listing 1979.

Jimi Hendrix '69 Flying V Custom (1991–1993): Based on 1969 model, mahogany body, 490R and 490T humbucking pickups, signature on pickguard, mahogany neck, split-diamond inlays, gold-plated hardware, first run of 400 numbered on truss-rod

cover, Hall of Fame series logo on back of peghead, Ebony finish.
Production: 25 promotional instruments for RCA Records.

Les Paul Classic Celebrity Series: Black finish, white pickguard, gold-plated hardware: July 1991.

Les Paul Classic Plus (1991–96, 1999–current): Figured maple top.

Les Paul Classic M-III electronics (1991–93): 1 humbucking and 2 single-coil pickups.

Les Paul Custom/400 (1991–92): Custom Shop model, Super 400-style slashed-block fingerboard inlay, Ebony or Antique White finish.

Les Paul Custom Black Beauty '54 Reissue (1991–current): Alnico V and P-90 pickups, Bigsby vibrato optional, Ebony finish.

Les Paul Custom Black Beauty '57 Reissue (1991–current): 2 or 3 humbucking pickups, Bigsby vibrato optional, Ebony finish.

Les Paul Custom Plus (1991–97): Figured maple top, Honeyburst, Dark Wine, Heritage Cherry Sunburst or Vintage Sunburst finish.

Les Paul Deluxe Hall of Fame Edition (1991): All gold finish.

Les Paul '59 Flametop Reissue (1991–current): See earlier listing 1958/1983.

Les Paul Studio Lite/lightly figured maple top (1991): limited run, 2-piece or 3-piece top of figured maple, 2 humbucking pickups with exposed coils, trapezoid inlays, Translucent Red or Translucent Amber finish.

Les Paul Studio Lite/M-III electronics (1991–94):

2 humbucking pickups and 1 single coil pickup, 2 knobs, 1 slide switch, 1 mini-switch.

SG Standard Celebrity Series (August 1991): Black finish, white knobs, white pickguard, gold-plated hardware.

Kalamazoo Award 100th Anniversary (1991): 2 made for Japan.

M-III Standard (1991–95)
Solidbody, swooping double cutaway with extended bass horn
- **Body & Hardware:** double-cutaway poplar solidbody, extended bass horn, Floyd Rose vibrato.
- **Neck:** 25½-inch scale, 24 frets, maple neck and fingerboard, black arrowhead inlay flush with bass side, peghead points to bass side, 6-on-a-side tuner arrangement with tuners all on treble side, logo reads upside down to player.
- **Pickups & Controls:** 2 ceramic magnet humbucking pickups with no covers in neck and bridge positions, NSX single-coil pickup with slug polepieces in middle position, 2-way toggle switch and 5-way slide switch for 10 pickup combinations.

M-III Deluxe (1991–92): Laminated body of maple/walnut/poplar, same electronics as M-III Standard, Floyd Rose vibrato, maple neck and fingerboard, arrowhead inlay flush with bass side, Antique Natural finish.

M-III-H (Standard) (1991–92): 2 humbucking pickups, no pickguard, Translucent Red or Translucent Amber finish.

M-III-H Deluxe (1991): 5-ply body with walnut top, curly maple back and poplar core, 2 humbucking pickups, 6-way switch, no pickguard, satin (non-gloss) neck finish, Antique Natural finish.

M-III Standard (1991–95): No pickguard, Translucent Red or Translucent Amber finish.

M-III Stealth (1991): Black limba wood body (similar to walnut), Floyd Rose vibrato, black chrome hardware, satin neck finish.

TF-7 (1991): No specs available, possibly 7-string.

30th Anniversary SG Custom (1991): Engraved *30th Anniversary* engraved on peghead inlay, TV Yellow finish (darker than traditional TV Yellow). Production: No more than 300.

'56 Les Paul Gold-top Reissue (1991–current): Reissue, soapbar P-90 pickups, Custom Authentic aging treatment optional from 2001, Vintage Original Spec aging treatment optional from 2006.

1958 Korina Flying V (1991–current) / 1959 Korina Flying V (1994–current): Replica of 1958 style, Korina body and neck, gold-plated hardware, Antique Natural finish.

1967 SG Custom (1991): Large 4-point pickguard, Wine Red finish.

1992

Chet Atkins SST 12-string Brett Michaels Edition (1992–93): See earlier listing 1990.
Chet Atkins SST 12-string Brett Michaels Edition (1992–93): Antique Gold finish. Production: 2.

Les Paul Anniversary (1992–93)
Single-cut solidbody, carved top, 40th Anniversary *at 12th fret*
- **Body & Hardware:** single-cutaway solidbody, carved top, gold-plated hardware, black finish.
- **Neck:** *40th Anniversary* engraved in 12th fret inlay.
- **Pickups & Controls:** 2 P-100 stacked coil

humbucking pickups with cream soapbar covers. Production: No more than 300.

Les Paul SG '67 Custom (1992–1993): Large 4-point pickguard, Wine Red or Classic White finish.

1993

Chet Atkins SST w/flame-top (1993–95): Flamed maple top, Antique Natural, Heritage Cherry Sunburst or Translucent Amber finish.

Chet Atkins Studio CE (1993–2000, 2004–05)
Single-cut solidbody acoustic, nylon strings, Chet Atkins signature on body
- **Body & Hardware:** single cutaway (deeper cutaway from 2004), hollow mahogany back (sound port from 2004), spruce top (cedar from 2004), no soundhole, flared bridge ends (moustache bridge from 2004), gold-plated hardware, Antique Natural finish.
- **Neck:** 26-inch scale, unbound ebony fingerboard with treble-side extension, 1¹³⁄₁₆-inch nut width, slotted peghead, decal logo.
- **Pickups & Controls:** under-saddle pickup, controls on rim (slider controls on circular plate on upper bass bout from 2004), individual string volume controls accessible internally, signature on upper bass bout near fingerboard, multiple-bound top with black outer layer.

Chet Atkins Studio CEC (1993–2000, 2004–05): 2-inch nut width.

Le Grand (1993–current): See earlier listing for Johnny Smith 1961.

Les Paul Classic Birdseye (1993): Birdseye maple top.

Les Paul Classic Premium Plus (1993–97): Highly figured maple top (flame runs all the way to the edge).

Les Paul Mahogany (1993)
Single-cut solidbody, carved mahogany top
- **Body & Hardware:** single-cutaway mahogany solidbody, carved top (no maple top).
- **Neck:** bound rosewood fingerboard, trapezoid inlays.
- **Pickups & Controls:** 2 P-90 pickups, 4 knobs, selector switch on upper bass bout.

Les Paul Standard Birdseye (1993–96): Birdseye maple top.

Les Paul SG '61 Reissue (1993–97): See earlier listing for Les Paul 1952.

Lonnie Mack Flying V (1993–94): Mahogany body, 1958-style control arrangement, Bigsby vibrato with anchor bar between lower bouts.

M-IV S Standard (1993–95): Steinberger vibrato, black chrome hardware, Ebony finish.

M-IV S Deluxe (1993–95): Steinberger vibrato, Natural finish.

Nighthawk Custom (1993–98)
Single-cut solidbody, strings through body, trapezoid inlay
- **Body & Hardware:** single cutaway, mahogany back, flat maple top, low profile bridge, strings through body, optional Floyd Rose vibrato (1994), gold-plated hardware, Antique Natural, Fireburst or Translucent Amber finish.
- **Neck:** 25½-inch scale, ebony fingerboard, trapezoid inlay.
- **Pickups & Controls:** 1 Firebird mini-humbucking pickup in neck position, 1 NSX single-coil pickup in middle position, 1 slant-mounted humbucking pickup, master volume, push/pull master tone, 5-way switch, optional 2-pickup version with no single-coil and no push/pull tone control.

Nighthawk Special (1993–98): Rosewood

fingerboard, dot inlays, gold-plated hardware, Ebony, Heritage Cherry or Vintage Sunburst finish.

Nighthawk Standard (1993–98): Rosewood fingerboard, double-parallelogram inlay, gold-plated hardware, optional 2-pickup version with no single-coil and no push/pull tone control, optional Floyd Rose vibrato (1994), Fireburst, Translucent Amber or Vintage Sunburst finish.

SG Standard Korina (1993–94): Korina (African limba wood) body, 3-piece sandwich body with rosewood center laminate, gold-plated hardware, Antique Natural finish. Production: 500.

Wes Montgomery Signature (1993–current)
Single-cut archtop, 1 humbucker
- **Body & Hardware:** 17-inch single-cutaway archtop, maple back and sides, carved spruce top, gold-plated hardware, Vintage Sunburst or Wine Red finish.
- **Neck:** bound ebony fingerboard, pearl block inlays.
- **Pickups & Controls:** 1 humbucking pickup in neck position.

1958 Korina Explorer (1993–current): Replica of 1958 version (5 with "split V" peghead shape), Korina body and neck, gold-plated hardware, Antique Natural finish.

1994

EDS-1275 Centennial (May 1994 guitar of the month): Ebony finish, serial number in raised numerals on tailpiece, numeral *1* of serial number formed by row of diamonds, letter *i* of logo dotted by inlaid diamond, gold medallion on back of peghead, gold-plated hardware, limited run of no more than 101 serial numbered from 1894–1994, package includes 16 x 20-inch framed photograph and gold signet ring.

ES-335 Centennial (Aug. 1994 guitar of the month): Cherry finish, serial number in raised numerals on tailpiece, numeral *1* of serial number formed by row of diamonds, letter *i* of logo dotted by inlaid diamond, gold medallion on back of peghead, gold-plated hardware, limited run of no more than 101 serial numbered from 1894–1994, packaged with 16 x 20-inch framed photograph and gold signet ring.

ES-350T Centennial (Mar. 1994 guitar of the month): Vintage Sunburst finish, serial number in raised numerals on tailpiece, numeral *1* of serial number formed by row of diamonds, letter *i* of logo dotted by inlaid diamond, gold medallion on back of peghead, gold-plated hardware, limited run of no more than 101 serial numbered from 1894–1994, package includes 16 x 20-inch framed photograph and gold signet ring.

ES-355 Centennial (June 1994 guitar of the month): Vintage Sunburst finish, serial number in raised numerals on tailpiece, numeral *1* of serial number formed by row of diamonds, letter *i* of logo dotted by inlaid diamond, gold medallion on back of peghead, gold-plated hardware, Vintage Sunburst finish, limited run of no more than 101 serial numbered from 1894–1994, package includes 16 x 20-inch framed photograph and gold signet ring.

Explorer Centennial (Apr. 1994 guitar of the month): Serial number in raised numerals on tailpiece, numeral *1* of serial number formed by row of diamonds, letter *i* of logo dotted by inlaid diamond, gold medallion on back of peghead, gold-plated hardware, Antique Gold finish, limited run of no more than 101 serial numbered from 1894–1994, package includes 16 x 20 framed photograph and gold signet ring.

Firebird VII Centennial (Sept. 1994 guitar of the month): Vintage Sunburst finish, serial number in raised numerals on tailpiece, numeral *1* of serial number formed by row of diamonds, letter *i* of logo dotted by inlaid diamond, gold medallion on back of

CUSTOM SHOP CREATIONS

Gibson's workshops have almost always been open to taking custom orders from artists or dealers, but only in recent decades has the notion of a self-contained 'Custom Shop' come to be. A Custom Shop of sorts existed in the Kalamazoo plant in the 1960s, and something more akin to the modern notion of the term was established in the Nashville factory between 1983–88.

The Custom Shop as it exists today got its start in 1993, however, when Gibson allocated a dedicated premises and staff to the operation in order to capitalize on the growing trend for models that were more finely crafted and a bit more special than the standard production guitars the leading manufacturers were turning out.

Over the course of the next ten years the Custom Shop – for a time referred to as Custom-Art-Historic – played a bigger and bigger part in Gibson's production, moving beyond special orders and 'art guitars' (one-off showpieces) to manufacture 'standard custom' models. Today Gibson Custom, as the department is known, offers a range of lines that are in continual production, although more limited than the standard production lines of Gibson USA.

The bulk of these fall under the umbrella of the Historic Series, which carries the standard-issue Custom reissue models (ie non-Signature or Limited Edition guitars). In 2006 the accuracy of these reproductions was cranked up a notch when Gibson morphed many Les Pauls and two early Les Paul/SGs from the Historic Series into the VOS (Vintage Original Spec) Series. At the time of writing, the VOS line included the '54 goldtop (still available, although not included in the catalog); '56 goldtop; '57 goldtop; two and three-pickup '57 Customs; '57 and '58 Les Paul Juniors; single and double-cutaway '60 Les Paul Specials; '58, '59 and '60 Sunburst Standards; and early-'60s-style SG Standard and Custom. While Gibson has tended to boast that each subsequent series of reissue models over the years has offered "the most accurate reproductions yet," as have so many makers, it seems the VOS Series really has landed squarely in that territory. A comprehensive list of revised specs helped to make these guitars more historically accurate, among them the use of a long-tenon neck joint, solid non-weight-relieved mahogany back (where applicable), accurate top-arch carve, vintage-style fret wire, correct headstock taper, historically correct binding, and more accurate pickup and control routings.

ES and archtop models fall under their own Custom Shop division, while reproductions of many Firebirds, the SG Special, the Flying V and Explorer are classified as 'Limited Models' under the SG/Designer heading. Alongside these, many more exclusive Custom Shop models appear in the 'Signature' and 'Inspired By' lines. The former offers, unsurprisingly, Signature models based on famous guitars played by the likes of Jimmy Page, Pete Townshend, Joe Perry and Neil Schon, while the latter carries models that are modified or hot-rodded according to the specifications of a range of artists. Among these are the Dave Grohl DG-335, Elliot Easton SG, Warren Haynes Model (a Les Paul Standard), Peter Frampton Les Paul Special, and others.

peghead, gold-plated hardware, limited run of no more than 101 serial numbered from 1894–1994, package includes 16 x 20 framed photograph and gold signet ring.

Flying V Centennial (July 1994 guitar of the month): Serial number in raised numerals on tailpiece, numeral *1* of serial number formed by row of diamonds, letter *i* of logo dotted by inlaid diamond, gold medallion on back of peghead, gold-plated hardware, Antique Gold finish, limited run of no more than 101 serial numbered from 1894–1994, package includes 16 x 20 framed photograph and gold signet ring.

Flying V Primavera (1994): Primavera wood (light mahogany), gold-plated hardware with Antique Natural finish, chrome-plated hardware with translucent and metallic finishes.

Les Paul '57 Black Beauty 3-Pickup Centennial (Nov. 1994 guitar of the month): 3 pickups, Ebony finish, serial number in raised numerals on tailpiece, numeral *1* of serial number formed by row of diamonds, letter *i* of logo dotted by inlaid diamond, gold medallion on back of peghead, gold-plated hardware, limited run of no more than 101 serial numbered from 1894–1994, package includes 16 x 20 framed photograph and gold signet ring.

Les Paul Special Double Cut Centennial (Jan. 1994 guitar of the month): Serial number in raised numerals on tailpiece, numeral *1* of serial number formed by row of diamonds, letter *i* of logo dotted by inlaid diamond, gold medallion on back of peghead, gold-plated hardware, Heritage Cherry finish, limited run of no more than 101 serial numbered from 1894–1994, package includes 16 x 20 framed photograph and gold signet ring.

Les Paul Special Single Cutaway Centennial (1994): Serial number in raised numerals on tailpiece, numeral *1* of serial number formed by row of diamonds, letter *i* of logo dotted by inlaid diamond, gold medallion on back of peghead, gold-plated hardware, gold or TV Yellow finish. Production: less than 10 prototypes only used for promotions.

Les Paul Standard Centennial (Oct. 1994 guitar of the month): Vintage Sunburst finish, limited serial number in raised numerals on tailpiece, numeral *1* of serial number formed by row of diamonds, letter *i* of logo dotted by inlaid diamond, gold medallion on

back of peghead, gold-plated hardware, run of no more than 101 serial numbered from 1894–1994, package includes 16 x 20 framed photograph and gold signet ring.

L-5CES Centennial (Dec. 1994 guitar of the month): Ebony finish, serial number in raised numerals on tailpiece, numeral *1* of serial number formed by row of diamonds, letter *i* of logo dotted by inlaid diamond, gold medallion on back of peghead, gold-plated hardware, limited run of no more than 101 serial numbered from 1894–1994, packaged with 16 x 20 framed photograph and gold signet ring.

'58 Les Paul Plain-top (1994–99, 2003–current): Plain maple top, Custom Authentic aging treatment optional from 2003, Vintage Original Spec aging treatment optional from 2006.

1959 Korina Flying V (1994–current): Replica of c1959 Flying V, see earlier listing 1958.

1995

All American I (1995–97) / **SG-X** (1998–2000)
SG body, 1 humbucker
- **Body & Hardware:** body & Hardware: solid mahogany double-cutaway body, pointed horns, Tune-o-matic bridge, chrome-plated hardware, Ebony finish.
- **Neck:** unbound rosewood fingerboard, dot inlays, decal logo.
- **Pickups & Controls:** 1 exposed-coil humbucking pickup 2 knobs, coil tap.

All American II (1995–97)
Double-cut solidbody, pointed horns (not as pointed as SG)
- **Body & Hardware:** double cutaway with pointed horns (not SG-shape, similar to early 1960s Melody Maker), vibrato, Ebony or Deep Wine Red finish.

- **Neck:** unbound rosewood fingerboard, dot inlays, *II* on truss-rod cover.
- **Pickups & Controls:** 2 oblong single-coil pickups with non-adjustable polepieces, 2 knobs, 1 switch.

Chet Atkins Super 4000 (1995, 1997)
Thinbody single-cut archtop, split-block inlays, floating pickup
- **Body & Hardware:** 18-inch archtop, carved spruce top, figured maple back and sides, Heritage Cherry Sunburst finish.
- **Neck:** 5-piece maple neck, ebony fingerboard, split-block inlays, 5-piece split-diamond peghead inlay.
- **Pickups & Controls:** floating full-size humbucking pickup.

Custom Shop ES-335 (1995–2001): Figured maple back, long pickguard, thick 1959-style neck, replica orange oval label.

Graceland (1995–96)
Thinbody acoustic guitar shape, ELVIS *on fingerboard*
- **Body & Hardware:** flat-top acoustic J-200 body shape, thin body, poplar back, spruce top, multiply top binding, Tune-o-matic bridge, pickguard with modern-art design from Elvis Presley's custom J-200 acoustic, gold-plated hardware.
- **Neck:** maple, bound ebony fingerboard, *ELVIS* and 2 stars inlaid on fingerboard.
- **Pickups & Controls:** 2 black soapbar pickups.

Jimmy Page Les Paul, 1st version (1995–99): Based on Page's 1959 Standard, push/pull knobs to control phasing and coil tapping, signature on pickguard, .050-inch fret height, Grover tuners with kidney-bean buttons (after approx. 500 shipped, frets lowered to .038-inch, locking nut added to bridge height-adjustment, Kluson tuners with keystone buttons), gold-plated hardware.

J-160E Montana Special (1995): No specifications available (similar to original J-160E, 1954).

Les Paul Bantam Elite (1995) / Les Paul Florentine Standard (1995–1997)
Single-cut solidbody, carved top, f-holes or diamond holes
- **Body & Hardware:** carved maple top, *f*-holes with Vintage Sunburst, Wine Red or black finish, diamond-shaped soundholes with sparkle finishes (sparkle finishes named Les Paul Elite Diamond Sparkle from 1995).
- **Neck:** ebony fingerboard, pearl block inlays, 5-piece split-diamond peghead inlay, gold-plated hardware.
- **Pickups & Controls:** 2 '57 Classic humbucking pickups.

Les Paul Bantam Elite Plus (1995) / Les Paul Florentine Standard Plus (1995–1998): Figured maple top, gold-plated hardware, Heritage Cherry Sunburst, Antique Natural or Emberglow finish standard, early examples also in purple, Emerald Green, Faded Blue, Midnight Blue, Rosa Red and Translucent Black finish.

Les Paul Elite Diamond Sparkle (1995–97): Diamond-shaped soundholes, sparkle (metalflake) gold, red or silver finish standard, early with Ice Blue, Brunswick Blue, black, copper or Lavender Sparkle finish.

Les Paul Standard Plus (1995–97): Figured maple top, Honeyburst, Heritage Cherry Sunburst or Vintage Sunburst finish.

Les Paul '60 Corvette (1995–97): Based on Les Paul Standard, top scooped out top to simulate side scoops on 1960 Chevrolet Corvette, *Corvette* stylized script inlay on fingerboard, crossed racing flags on peghead, Cascade Green, Tuxedo Black, Horizon Blue, Roman Red, Sateen Silver or Ermine White finish.

Les Paul '63 Corvette Sting Ray (1995–97): Based on SG, maple body and neck top carved to resemble back split-window of 1963 Chevrolet Corvette Stingray, 1 humbucking pickup with no polepieces ebony fingerboard, *Sting Ray* inlay, crossed racing flags on peghead, nickel-plated hardware, Riverside Red, silver or black finish.

1996

BluesHawk (1996–2003)
Single-cut solidbody, Varitone rotary control, diamond inlay

- **Body & Hardware:** single cutaway, mahogany back, flat maple top, semihollow poplar body, *f*-holes, Maestro Bigsby-style optional 1998.
- **Neck:** 25½-inch scale, unbound rosewood fingerboard, diamond inlay, stacked-diamond peghead inlay, pearl logo, gold-plated hardware, Ebony or Cherry finish.
- **Pickups & Controls:** 2 special Blues 90 pickups with cream soapbar covers and non-adjustable poles, 2 knobs (with push/pull to disable Varitone), slide switch, 6-position Vari-tone control, combination bridge/tailpiece with individual string adjustments, strings through body, single-bound top.

ES-5 Reissue (1996–2006): 3 P-90 pickups.

ES-336 (1996–98) / **CS-336** (2002–current)
Thinbody double-cut archtop, smaller than ES-335, dot inlays

- **Body & Hardware:** 13½-inch double-cutaway semi-hollowbody, routed mahogany back with solid center area, arched (routed) maple top available with plain or figured grain, *f*-holes, rounded double cutaways, body lines similar to ES-335, back beveled on bass side, Tune-o-matic bridge, bound top and back, chrome-plated hardware.
- **Neck:** offset-V neck profile, bound rosewood fingerboard with compound radius, dot inlays, tapered peghead with straight string-pull (standard peghead from 2002), decal logo, Custom Shop decal logo on peghead, sealed-back tuners, inked-on serial number.
- **Pickups & Controls:** 2 '57 Classic humbucking pickups, 4 knobs.

Futura Reissue (1996) / **Mahogany Futura** (2002–04)
Angular body, V-shaped peghead (reissue of Explorer prototype)

- **Body & Hardware:** mahogany body, body shape similar to Explorer but with sharper angles and narrower treble horn
- **Neck:** unbound rosewood fingerboard, dot inlays, V-shaped peghead.
- **Pickups & Controls:** 2 humbucking pickups, 3 knobs.

Production: 100 (1996); 15 in each of four metallic colors (2002–2004).

Joe Perry Les Paul (1996–2000): Curly maple top, no binding, pearloid pickguard and truss-rod cover, unbound rosewood fingerboard, trapezoid inlays, specially wound bridge pickup, push/pull tone control to activate mid-boost, master tone control, Translucent Blackburst stain finish.

J-160E Yamano Reissue (1996): Made for Japan distribution only.

Landmark (1996–97)
Single-cut solidbody, flat top, strings through body, Firebird mini-humbuckers

- **Body & Hardware:** single cutaway, mahogany back, flat maple top, low profile bridge, strings through body, bound top, combination bridge/tailpiece with individual string adjustments.
- **Neck:** 25½-inch scale, unbound rosewood fingerboard, dot inlays, pearl logo, gold-plated hardware, Glacier Blue, Sequoia Red, Mojaveburst, Navajo Turquoise or Everglades Green finish.

- **Pickups & Controls:** 2 Firebird mini-humbucking pickups, 2 knobs, 3-way slide switch with coil-tap capability.

Les Paul Catalina (1996–97)
Single-cut solidbody, carved top, Custom Shop inlay on peghead
- **Body & Hardware:** single-cutaway solidbody, carved maple top, Tune-o-matic bridge, nickel-plated hardware, Pearl Black, Canary Yellow or Riverside Red finish.
- **Neck:** ebony fingerboard with compound radius, pearl trapezoid inlays, pearl Custom Shop logo inlay on peghead.
- **Pickups & Controls:** 2 humbucking pickups, 4 knobs, selector switch on upper bass bout.

Les Paul Elegant (1996–current)
Single-cut solidbody, carved top, abalone fingerboard and peghead inlay
- **Body & Hardware:** highly flamed maple top, nickel-plated hardware, Heritage Darkburst or Firemist finish.
- **Neck:** ebony fingerboard with compound radius, abalone trapezoid inlays, abalone Custom Shop peghead inlay.
- **Pickups & Controls:** 2 humbucking pickups, 4 knobs, selector switch on upper bass bout.

Les Paul Smartwood (Standard) (1996–99)
Single-cut solidbody, carved top, bound top, green leaf on truss-rod cover
- Les Paul Standard with wood certified by the Rainforest Alliance, gold-plated hardware, Natural finish.
- Chechen fingerboard, pearl trapezoid inlays, green leaf on truss-rod cover.
- **Pickups & Controls:** 2 humbucking pickups, 4 knobs, selector switch on upper bass bout.

Les Paul Studio Gem (1996–97): 2 P-90 cream soapbar pickups, rosewood fingerboard, trapezoid inlays, *Studio* on truss-rod cover, pearl logo, gold-

plated hardware, Ruby Red, Emerald Green, Topaz Yellow, Sapphire Blue or Amethyst Purple finish.

Les Paul Tie-Dye (1996)
Single-cut solidbody, tie-dye top
- Top hand-finished by artist George St. Pierre in simulated tie-dyed pattern.
- **Neck:** bound rosewood fingerboard, trapezoid inlays.
- **Pickups & Controls:** 2 humbucking pickups, 4 knobs.
Production: 103.

Les Paul Ultima (1996–current)
Single-cut solidbody, carved top, elaborate fingerboard inlay
- Highly flamed maple top, abalone top border, trapeze tailpiece.
- Optional fingerboard inlay patterns of flame, tree of life or harp (from an early Gibson harp guitar fingerboard inlay), pearl tuner buttons, gold-plated hardware, Heritage Cherry Sunburst finish.
- **Pickups & Controls:** 2 humbucking pickups, 4 knobs, selector switch on upper bass bout.

L-5 Studio (1996–current)
Single-cut archtop, black binding, dot inlays
- **Body & Hardware:** 17-inch wide maple body, rounded cutaway, solid carved spruce top, Tune-o-matic bridge, trapeze tailpiece, "ice cube marble" pattern celluloid pickguard, black binding on top and back, Translucent Blue or Translucent Red finish.
- **Neck:** unbound ebony fingerboard, dot inlays, pearl logo.
- **Pickups & Controls:** 2 humbucking pickups, 4 knobs, switch on cutaway bout.

M-III (1996–97): Mahogany body, 3 humbucking pickups, Ebony or Wine Red finish.

Switchmaster Reissue (1996–2006): 3 humbucking pickups.

Switchmaster Reissue Alnico (1996–2006):
3 Alnico V pickups.

The Hawk (1996–97)
Single-cut solidbody, Hawk on truss-rod cover
- **Body & Hardware:** Nighthawk body shape, single cutaway mahogany solidbody (no top cap), no binding, Ebony or Wine Red finish.
- **Neck:** 25½-inch scale, unbound rosewood fingerboard, dot inlays, model name on truss-rod cover, American flag decal on back of peghead.
- **Pickups & Controls:** 2 humbucking pickups, 2 knobs, 1 switch.

The Paul II (1996–97) / **The Paul II SL** (Sans Lacquer) (1998):
Thin single-cut solidbody, The Paul II on truss-rod cover
- 3-piece thin mahogany body (not sandwich), carved top, no binding, Tune-o-matic bridge, Ebony or Wine Red finish (SL urethane finish specified but not on all examples 1998).
- **Neck:** unbound rosewood fingerboard, dot inlays, model name on truss-rod cover, decal logo.
- 2 exposed-coil humbucking pickups, 4 knobs, selector switch on upper bass bout.

'54 Les Paul Gold-top Reissue (1996–current):
Soapbar P-90 pickups, wraparound bridge, gold-top finish, Vintage Original Spec aging treatment optional from 2006.

'58 Les Paul Figured Top (1996–99, 2001–03):
Less top figuration than Flametop Reissue but more than '58 Plain-top, Custom Authentic aging treatment optional from 2001.

1997

Ace Frehley Les Paul (1997–2001): 3 DiMarzio pickups, multiple-bound top, lightning bolt inlay, signature at 12th fret, bound peghead with Ace graphic, Heritage Cherry Sunburst finish.

ES-346 (1997–98) / **Paul Jackson Jr ES-346** (1999–2006)
Thinbody double-cut archtop, smaller than ES-335, double-parallelogram inlay
- **Body & Hardware:** 13½-inch double-cutaway semi-hollowbody, routed mahogany back with solid center area, arched (routed) maple top available with plain or figured grain, ƒ-holes, rounded double cutaways, body lines similar to ES-335, back beveled on bass side, Tune-o-matic bridge, bound top and back, gold-plated hardware, Emberglow, faded Cherry or Gingerburst finish.
- **Neck:** offset-V neck profile, bound rosewood fingerboard with compound radius, double-parallelogram inlay, tapered peghead with straight string-pull, pearl logo, Custom Shop decal logo on peghead, sealed-back tuners, chrome-plated hardware, inked-on serial number.
- **Pickups & Controls:** 2 '57 Classic humbucking pickups, 4 knobs.

Generation Swine SG Special (mid 1997):
Promotional guitars for Motley Crue's *Generation Swine* CD and tour, Ebony finish, red pickguard with "Generation Swine" logo. Production: 5 given away at Guitar Center stores, 1 given away nationally.

Les Paul Custom Shop Standard (1997–98):
1 zebra-coil pickup, 1 black-coil pickup, no pickup covers, Grover tuners, faded Cherry Sunburst finish, inked-on serial number.

Les Paul DC Pro (1997–98, 2006–current)
Double-cut solidbody, carved top, trapezoid inlays, crown peghead inlay
- **Body & Hardware:** double-cutaway body shape like 1959 Les Paul Jr, rounded horns, carved highly figured maple top, weight-relieved mahogany back, Tune-o-matic or wraparound bridge, nickel-plated hardware.
- **Neck:** 24¾-inch or 25½-inch scale, unbound rosewood fingerboard, aged trapezoid inlays, tapered peghead for straight string-pull (standard

peghead shape for 2006), crown peghead inlay (no Les Paul silkscreen).
- **Pickups & Controls:** 2 humbucking pickups or 2 P-90 white soapbar pickups (P-90s with wraparound bridge only, humbuckers only from 2006), 2 knobs, 1 switch.

Les Paul DC Studio (1997–98)
Double-cut solidbody, carved top, dot inlays, 2 knobs
- **Body & Hardware:** double-cutaway body shape like 1959 Les Paul Jr, rounded horns, carved maple top, wraparound bridge (Tune-o-matic 1998), unbound top and back, chrome-plated hardware, Ebony, Heritage Cherry Sunburst, Emerald Green or Ruby finish.
- **Neck:** 24¾-inch scale, unbound rosewood fingerboard, dot inlays, standard peghead shape.
- **Pickups & Controls:** 2 humbucking pickups, 2 knobs.

Les Paul Elegant Quilt (1997): Quilted maple top.

Les Paul Elegant Double Quilt (1997): Quilted maple top, figured mahogany back.

Les Paul Elegant Super Double Quilt (1997): Highly quilted maple top, highly figured mahogany back, Antique Natural or Butterscotch finish.

Les Paul Korina (1997)
Single-cut solidbody, carved top, Korina back and neck (looks like light mahogany)
- **Body & Hardware:** single-cutaway solidbody, carved figured maple top, Korina (African limba wood) back, nickel-plated hardware.
- **Neck:** Korina neck.
- **Pickups & Controls:** 2 humbucking pickups, 4 knobs.

Les Paul Mahogany Custom (1997): 1-piece mahogany body with carved top, 3 '57 Classic humbucking pickups, gold-plated hardware, faded Cherry finish.

Les Paul/SG Custom Reissue (1997–2005): See earlier entry 1963.

'54 Les Paul Oxblood (1997–2003): '57 Classic humbuckers with exposed black coils, wraparound bridge, Oxblood finish.

'57 Les Paul Gold-top Mary Ford (1997–current): '57 Reissue with ES-295 style gold leaves stenciled on pickguard, custom armrest on lower bass bout, 2 humbucking pickups, gold-top finish.

Slash Les Paul (1997): Slash image carved into top, Cranberry finish.
Production: 50.

Wes Montgomery Heart (1997): Reissue of one of Wes Montgomery's personal L-5s, heart-shaped pearl inlay with engraved *Wes Montgomery* in cutaway bout, special leather case, certificate.
Production: 25.

1998

Byrdland Florentine (1998–current): Pointed cutaway.

ES-135 Gothic (1998–99): 2 humbucking pickups with no covers, black pickguard, ebony fingerboard, moon-and-star inlay at 12th fret, no other inlay, white outline of logo on peghead, black chrome hardware, flat black finish.

ES-335 Block (1998–2000): Unbound ebony fingerboard, small block inlays.

ES-335 Gothic (1998): 2 '57 Classic humbucking pickups with no covers, black pickguard, ebony fingerboard, moon-and-star inlay at 12th fret, no other inlay, white outline of logo on peghead, black chrome hardware, flat black finish.

ACCESS ALL FRETS: LES PAUL GOES DOUBLE-CUT

Having been subject to a range of updates over the years, the classic Les Paul design received what was arguably its most significant modification in 40 years with the release of the Les Paul DC Pro in 1997. The guitar featured two humbuckers (P-90s optional) and the carved maple top and mahogany back (although now weight-relieved, courtesy of a series of unseen chambers) that have come to characterize the breed, but an extra sweep of the saw gave it a second cutaway, resulting in a new yet somehow very familiar dual-horned design. The slightly more rounded and very slightly asymmetrical cutaway horns followed an outline closer to those of the double-cutaway Les Paul Junior and Special circa 1960, and the design was further streamlined by moving the selector switch down to the lower bout and including only master volume and tone controls, rather than the individual controls of the Les Paul Standard. Alongside the DC Pro, Gibson released the Les Paul DC Studio, which followed the low-frills theme of the Les Paul Studio released in 1983. The following year the short-lived Les Paul DC Standard joined the lineup.

Double-cutaway Les Paul-style guitars from other makers had been popular since the 1970s, most notably perhaps from makers Hamer and Yamaha, so this would seem an obvious and long-overdue arrival from Gibson with the aim of squelching the competition. The timing of the Les Paul DC range was probably inspired more by the success of Paul Reed Smith guitars, however, whose double-cutaway but otherwise fairly Les Paul-ish models had carved out a big share of the marketplace for themselves. In fact, the outline of the DC's body most closely resembled that of PRS's Santana model, still a special-order instrument at that time. After PRS issued its own Singlecut model in 2000, which had a single-cutaway body that more closely resembled the classic Les Paul body lines, Gibson filed a lawsuit claiming trademark infringement against the Les Paul. After initially being upheld by the court in Nashville, with an order handed down for PRS to stop sales of the Singlecut, the decision was eventually reversed and Gibson's final appeal denied by the United States Supreme Court in June 2006.

1986

Explorer Gothic (1998–2001) / **X-Plorer Gothic** (2001): No pickup covers, black pickguard, ebony fingerboard, moon-and-star inlay at 12th fret (no other inlay), white-outline headstock logo, black chrome hardware, flat black finish.

Flying V '98 (1998): 2 ceramic-magnet humbucking pickups with exposed coils, 1958-style controls (3-in-line knob configuration, switch above knobs, jack in lower treble bout), Grover tuners with metal buttons, Natural or Naturalburst finish with gold-plated hardware or Translucent Purple finish with chrome-plated hardware.

Flying V '98 Gothic (1998–2001): 2 '57 Classic humbucking pickups with no covers, Flying V '98 control configuration with 3-in-line knobs, black pickguard, ebony fingerboard, moon-and-star inlay at 12th fret, no other inlay, white outline of logo on peghead, black chrome hardware, satin Ebony finish.

John Lennon J-160E Bed-In (1998): Based on Lennon's stripped 1963, with line drawing of Lennon and Yoko Ono on top. Production: 47 sets (sold with Fab Four Magical Tour and Bed-In models).

John Lennon J-160E Fab Four (1998): Based on 1963 version, Sunburst finish. Production: 47 sets (sold with Magical Tour and Bed-In models).

John Lennon J-160E Magical Tour (1998): Based on Lennon's custom-painted 1963, with purple, blue and red swirl-pattern finish. Production: 47 sets (sold with Fab Four and Bed-In models).

Les Paul DC Standard (Les Paul Standard-DC) (1998)
Double-cut solidbody, carved top, trapezoid inlays, no ornamental peghead inlay
- **Body & Hardware:** double-cutaway body shape like 1959 Les Paul Jr, rounded horns, carved flame maple top, Tune-o-matic bridge, unbound top, unbound back, chrome- or gold-plated hardware, translucent finish colors: Amber Serrano, Blue Diamond, Black Pepper, Red Hot Tamale or Green Jalapeno; limited edition finish colors: Tangerineburst or Lemonburst.
- **Neck:** bound rosewood fingerboard, trapezoid inlays, standard peghead shape, pearl logo, no Les Paul designation on peghead or truss-rod cover.
- **Pickups & Controls:** 2 humbucking pickups, 2 knobs, switch near bridge, 24¾-inch scale.

Les Paul Smartwood Exotic (1998–2002)
Thin single-cut solidbody, carved top, green leaf on truss-rod cover, dot inlays
- **Body & Hardware:** thinsingle cutaway (like The Paul II) with body of exotic wood certified by the Rainforest Alliance, mahogany back, top cap options include curupay, taperyva guasu, cancharana, peroba, banara or ambay guasu, gold-plated hardware, SL (Sans Lacquer) matte polyurethane finish specified.
- **Neck:** curupay fingerboard, dot inlays, green leaf on truss-rod cover.
- **Pickups & Controls:** 2 humbucking pickups, 2 knobs, 1 switch.

Les Paul Special SL (Sans Lacquer) (1998): Single cutaway, 2 black soapbar P-100 pickups, urethane finish specified, many with lacquer.

Old Hickory Les Paul (1998)

Single-cut solidbody, carved top, Andrew Jackson on peghead
- **Body & Hardware:** tulip poplar body from 274-year-old tree on the grounds of The Hermitage (Andrew Jackson's residence in Nashville) felled by a tornado on April 16, 1998, image of The Hermitage on pickguard, multiply binding.
- **Neck:** hickory fingerboard, *Old Hickory* pearl fingerboard inlay, Andrew Jackson's image on peghead inlay (same image as on a $20 bill).
- **Pickups & Controls:** 2 humbucking pickups, 4 knobs.
Production: Less than 200.

SG-Z (1998)
Double-cut solidbody, pointed horns, Z-shaped tailpiece
- **Body & Hardware:** double cutaway with pointed horns, Tune-o-matic bridge, Z-shaped tailpiece with strings through body, small pickguard.
- **Neck:** bound rosewood fingerboard, split-diamond inlay, 3-piece reverse-Z pearl peghead inlay, black chrome hardware, platinum or verdigris finish.
- **Pickups & Controls:** 1 stacked-coil and 1 standard humbucking pickup, 2 knobs, selector switch between knobs.

Tony Iommi Les Paul SG (1998, 2001–05): 2 custom-wound humbucking pickups with no polepieces, ebony fingerboard, iron cross inlays, chrome-plated hardware, left-handed or right-handed, Ebony finish.

1957 Les Paul Jr Double Cutaway (1998–99): Nickel-plated hardware.

1957 Les Paul Jr Single Cutaway (1998–current): Nickel-plated hardware, Vintage Original Spec aging treatment optional from 2006.

1960 Les Paul Special Single Cutaway (1998–current): 2 black soapbar P-100 pickups,

Vintage Original Spec aging treatment optional from 2006.

1999

B.B. King "Little Lucille" (1999–current)
Single-cut solidbody, pointed horn, Little Lucille *on top*
- **Body & Hardware:** semi-hollow poplar body, flat top, *f*-holes, TP-6 fine-tune tailpiece, gold-plated truss-rod cover engraved with *B.B. King,* black finish, *Little Lucille* on upper bass bout next to fingerboard, black finish.
- **Neck:** 25½-inch scale, unbound rosewood fingerboard, diamond inlay, stacked-diamond peghead inlay, pearl logo.
- **Pickups & Controls:** 2 special design Blues 90 pickups with cream soapbar covers and non-adjustable poles, 2 knobs (with push/pull to disable Varitone), slide switch, 6-position Vari-tone control.

Dale Earnhardt Les Paul (1999–2001): Based on single-cutaway Les Paul Special, top overlay with graphic by Sam Bass, hood pins, lug nut control knobs, Simpson racing harness strap, chrome-plated hardware, ebony fingerboard, signature inlay, Ebony finish. Production: 333.

ES-335 Dot (1999–current): See earlier listing 1958.

Les Paul Junior Lite (1999–2002): Double cutaway, contoured back, Tune-o-matic bridge, unbound rosewood fingerboard, mini-trapezoid (½-scale) inlay, *Les Paul Special* silkscreen on peghead, 2 P-100 stacked humbucking pickups, 4 knobs, selector switch near bridge.

Les Paul Jr Special (1999–2001): Single cutaway, contoured back on bass side, Tune-o-matic bridge, unbound rosewood fingerboard, mini-trapezoid inlay (½-scale), 2 P-100 stacked-coil humbucking pickups, selector switch on upper bass bout.

Les Paul Standard Lite (1999–current)
Single-cut solidbody, carved top, ¾-scale trapezoid inlays
- **Body & Hardware:** double-cutaway body shape like 1959 Les Paul Jr, rounded horns, no binding, gold-plated hardware, Translucent Amber, Translucent Red or Translucent Blue finish.
- **Neck:** rosewood fingerboard, medium (¾-scale) trapezoid inlays, no Les Paul designation on peghead or truss-rod cover.
- **Pickups & Controls:** 2 humbucking pickups with covers.

Pat Martino Custom / Pat Martino Signature (1999–2006)
Thinbody single-cut archtop, no fingerboard inlay, curly top
- **Body & Hardware:** 16-inch thin semi-hollowbody, single pointed cutaway, carved flamed maple top, routed mahogany back, *f*-holes, Tune-o-matic bridge, stopbar tailpiece, Caramel or Heritage Cherry Sunburst finish.
- **Neck:** mahogany, bound ebony fingerboard, no inlay, narrow peghead with straight string-pull, pearl logo.
- **Pickups & Controls:** 2 humbucking pickups, 4 knobs, selector switch on upper bass bout.

Pat Martino Standard (1999–2000): Plain maple top, Ebony or Vintage Red finish.

Paul Jackson Jr ES-346 (1999–2006): See earlier entry for ES-346 1997.

SG Classic (1999–2001)
Double-cut solidbody, pointed horns, 2 pickups, Classic *on truss-rod cover*
- **Body & Hardware:** double-cutaway mahogany solidbody, pointed horns, Tune-o-matic bridge, large pickguard.
- **Neck:** bound rosewood fingerboard, dot inlays.
- **Pickups & Controls:** 2 P-90 pickups, 4 knobs.

SG Special Gothic (1999–2000 / **SG Gothic** (2001–02): 2 exposed-coil humbuckers, satin Ebony finish, ebony fingerboard, moon-and-star inlay at 12th fret (no other inlay), black hardware.

SG Supreme (1999–2004 2007–current) / **SG Supreme '57 Humbucker** (2005–2006)
Double-cut solidbody, pointed horns, curly maple top, split-diamond inlays
- **Body & Hardware:** double cutaway with pointed horns, mahogany back, flamed maple top cap, gold-plated hardware, Fireburst (3-tone Sunburst shaded from bottom of body to horns) finish.
- **Neck:** bound ebony fingerboard, split-diamond inlay, bound peghead , 5-piece split-diamond (SG Custom style) peghead inlay.
- **Pickups & Controls:** 2 P-90A soapbar pickups with black covers ('57 Classic humbuckers from 2005), 4 knobs.

Swingmaster ES-135 (1999): 2 dog-ear P-90 pickups, ebony fingerboard, pearloid trapezoid inlays, optional Bigsby vibrato, Custom Coral, Daddy-O Yellow, Mint Green or Outa-Sight White finish.

Swingmaster ES-175 (1999): 2 P-90 pickups, ebony fingerboard, pearloid trapezoid inlays, optional Bigsby vibrato, Custom Coral, Daddy-O Yellow, Mint Green or Outa-Sight White finish.

Web-Slinger One (1999): Spiderman graphic, mahogany body, single cutaway, ebony fingerboard, web-pattern inlay. Production: 75 signed by Stan Lee, 75 signed by John Romita Sr.

Zakk Wylde Custom (Bottle Cap) (1999, 2002): Bottle caps on top of guitar.

2000

Angus Young Signature SG (2000–current): Based on SG Standard, large pickguard, 2 humbucking

pickups (1 custom wound), Maestro vibrato with lyre and logo engraved in cover, "devil signature" ornament on peghead, nickel-plated hardware, aged Cherry finish.

Chet Atkins CEC – True Cedar (2000–2005): Cedar top, ebony fingerboard, 2-inch wide at nut, Natural finish.

Chet Atkins SST – True Cedar (2000–2005): Cedar top, Natural finish.

Dale Earnhardt "The Intimidator" Les Paul (2000–01): Based on single-cutaway Les Paul Special, top overlay with graphic by Sam Bass, silver finish with black drawings and red trim, The Intimidator inlaid on fingerboard, 3 inlaid on peghead. Production: 333.

Gary Moore Les Paul (2000–01): Flamed maple top, no binding, 2 exposed-coil humbucking pickups with reverse-wound zebra-coil in neck position, unbound fingerboard, pearl trapezoid inlay, Lemonburst finish.

Jim Beam Les Paul (2000–03): Features from Jim Beam whiskey.

Les Paul Classic Mahogany Top (2000): Mahogany top cap, long neck tenon, 2 exposed-coil zebra-coil humbuckers.

Les Paul Standard Raw Power (2000–2001): Chrome-plated hardware, satin Natural finish.

Les Paul Standard Sparkle Top (2000): Frost, Sterling or Crimson Sparkle finish.

Les Paul Studio Gothic (2000–01): 2 exposed-coil humbuckers, satin Ebony finish, ebony fingerboard, moon-and-star inlay at 12th fret (no other inlay), black hardware.

Peter Frampton Les Paul (2000–current):

3 exposed-coil pickups wired so that middle pickup is always on, Les Paul custom trim, weight-relieved body, maple top, Antiqued binding, signature at 12th fret, Ebony finish.

Pete Townshend Ltd Edition SG Special (2000)
Double-cut solidbody, pointed horns, dot inlays, Custom Shop production.
- **Body & Hardware:** solid mahogany dual-cutaway body with pointed horns, wide late-'60s scratchplate, wrapover bridge.
- **Neck:** mahogany neck with bound rosewood fingerboard, dot inlays.
- **Pickups & Controls:** 2 black soapbar P-90 pickups, 4 knobs, 1 switch.

SG/Les Paul with Deluxe Lyre Vibrato (2000–2002): Vibrato with lyre and logo on coverplate.

Zakk Wylde Bullseye Les Paul (2000–current): Painted bullseye (Mylar appliqué optional 2002) EMG humbucking pickups with black covers, ebony fingerboard, pearl block inlays, 5-piece split-diamond peghead inlay, gold-plated tuners.

Zakk Wylde Rough Top Les Paul (2000–02): Unfinished roughed-up top.

30th Anniversary Les Paul Deluxe (2000): Ebony, Wine Red or Bullion Gold finish.

'57 LP Gold-top Darkback Reissue (2000–current): Dark-stained back, Vintage Original Spec aging treatment optional from 2006.

1958 Les Paul Jr Double Cutaway (2000–current): Nickel plated hardware, Vintage Original Spec aging treatment optional from 2006.

1963 Firebird I (2000–current): See earlier listing 1963.

1964 Firebird III (2000–current): See earlier listing 1963.

1964 Firebird V (Custom Shop, 2000–current): See earlier listing 1963.

1965 Firebird VII (Custom Shop 2000–current): See earlier listing 1963.

2001

Andy Summers 1960 ES-335 (2001): Replica of Summers' personal guitar, 1960 specs, aged Cherry finish.
Production: 50.

Dale Earnhardt Jr Les Paul (2001): Based on single-cutaway Les Paul Special, graphics include #8 race car, signature and Bud logo, ebony fingerboard with inlaid signature, Earnhardt Red finish.
Production: 333.

Dickey Betts Ultra Aged 1957 Les Paul Gold-top (2001–2003): Scarfed back, concho-style jackplate and switch washer.
Production: 114.

J-190EC Super Fusion (2001–04)
Acoustic flat-top, rounded cutaway, 3 knobs
- **Body & Hardware:** 16-inch wide acoustic flat top, rounded cutaway, moustache bridge.
- **Neck:** bound ebony fingerboard, slashed-block inlays, 5-piece slashed-diamond peghead inlay, pearl logo.
- **Pickups & Controls:** 1 single-coil pickup mounted at end of bridge, 1 under-saddle pickup, 3 knobs, selector switch on upper bass bout.

Lenny Kravitz 1967 Flying V (2001–04): Mirror pickguard, black finish with sparkles, maestro vibrato.
Production: 125.

Les Paul Acoustic (2001–02) / **Les Paul Acoustic Plain-top** (2003–05)
Single-cut solidbody, carved top, undersaddle pickup
- **Body & Hardware:** single-cutaway solidbody,

carved top of figured maple (plain-top from 2003), no binding, strings through body.
- **Neck:** unbound rosewood fingerboard, trapezoid inlays, Les Paul silkscreen on peghead, pearl logo.
- **Pickups & Controls:** piezo pickup under bridge, controls on rim.

Les Paul Class 5 (2001–current)
Single-cut solidbody, carved top, figured top, lightweight body
- **Body & Hardware:** single-cutaway solidbody, carved maple top (figured top 2003–04, quilt top 2003–current), weight-relieved mahogany back.
- **Neck:** bound rosewood fingerboard, '60s slim-taper neck profile, pearloid trapezoid inlays, Les Paul silkscreen on peghead, long neck tenon.
- **Pickups & Controls:** 2 humbucking pickups, 4 knobs, selector switch on upper bass bout.

Les Paul/SG Standard Reissue (2001–03) / **SG Standard** (Custom shop version 2004–current): reissue of early 1960s version, does not say *Les Paul* anywhere, small pickguard, nickel-plated hardware, optional Maestro vibrato, aged hardware optional 2001–05, Vintage Original Spec or Custom Authentic aging treatment optional from 2006.

Les Paul Standard Doublecut Plus (2001–current): Figured top, chambered body, 2 knobs, gold-plated hardware, "Standard" on truss-rod cover, Les Paul signature silkscreen on peghead, transparent finishes.

Les Paul Junior Special Plus (2001–05): Flat curly maple top cap, two humbucking pickups, gold-plated hardware, decal logo.

Les Paul/SG Special Reissue (2001–03) / **SG Special** (Custom Shop version 2004–current): Reissue of early 1960s version, wraparound bridge, small pickguard, 2 soapbar P-90s, nickel-plated hardware, Maestro vibrato optional 2001–05, Vintage Original Spec aging treatment optional from 2006.

L-5 Signature (2001–05)
Single-cut archtop, rounded horn, scaled-down L-5
- **Body & Hardware:** 15½-inch single-cutaway archtop, 2⅝-inch deep, rounded cutaway, Tune-o-matic bridge, multiply top binding, single-bound back, gold-plated hardware.
- **Neck:** 25½-inch scale, bound ebony fingerboard, pearl block inlays, flowerpot peghead inlay.
- **Pickups & Controls:** 2 humbucking pickups.

Pete Townshend Signature SG Special (2001)
Double-cut solidbody, pointed horns, dot inlays.
- **Body & Hardware:** solid mahogany dual-cutaway body with pointed horns, wide late-'60s scratchplate, wrapover bridge.
- **Neck:** mahogany neck with bound rosewood fingerboard, dot inlays.
- **Pickups & Controls:** 2 black soapbar P-90 pickups, 4 knobs, 1 switch.

Playboy 2001 Playmate of the Year (2001): Based on Les Paul Standard, Pinkburst finish. Production: 50.

SG Gothic (2001–02): See earlier listing for SG Special Gothic 1999.

Steve Howe Signature ES-175 (2001–current): Based on Howe's 1964, multiply top binding, pearl-inlaid ebony bridge base, zigzag tailpiece, nickel-plated hardware.

X-Men Wolverine Les Paul (2001): X-men graphic finish. Production: 50.

2002

Bob Marley Les Paul Special (2002–03): Based on c1972 model (never catalogued), single cutaway, aluminum pickguard and elliptical switch washer, 2 soapbar P-90 pickups, selector switch on upper bass bout, small block inlays, wide binding on

peghead, aged Cherry finish appears stripped.
Production: 200.

Dickey Betts '57 Redtop Les Paul (2002–03): 1957
Les Paul Standard specs, 2 humbuckers, red top
finish.
Production: 55.

ES-137 Classic (2002–current)
*Thinbody single-cut archtop, pointed horn, trapezoid
inlays*
- **Body & Hardware:** 16-inch laminated
  maple/poplar/maple semi-hollowbody, 2¼-inch
  deep, pointed cutaway, *f*-holes, Tune-o-matic
  bridge, multiply top binding, single-bound back,
  chrome- or gold-plated hardware.
- **Neck:** maple, bound rosewood fingerboard,
  trapezoid inlays, *C* inlay at 12th fret, decal logo.
- **Pickups & Controls:** 2 humbucking pickups,
  4 knobs, selector switch on upper bass bout.

ES-137 Custom (2002–current)
*Thinbody single-cut archtop, pointed horn, split-
diamond inlays*
- **Body & Hardware:** 16-inch laminated
  maple/poplar/maple semi-hollowbody, 2¼-inch
  deep, pointed cutaway, *f*-holes, Tune-o-matic
  bridge, multiply top binding, single-bound back,
  chrome- or gold-plated hardware.
- **Neck:** 3-piece maple neck, bound ebony
  fingerboard, trapezoid inlays, pearl logo.
- **Pickups & Controls:** 2 humbucking pickups,
  4 knobs, rotary Varitone switch, selector switch
  on upper bass bout.

ES-137P (Premier) (2002–04)
*Thinbody single-cut archtop, pointed horn, half-
trapezoid inlays*
- **Body & Hardware:** 16-inch laminated
  maple/poplar/maple semi-hollowbody, 2¼-inch
  deep, pointed cutaway, *f*-holes, Tune-o-matic
  bridge, black body binding, chrome-plated
  hardware, metallic finishes.

- **Neck:** maple, unbound rosewood fingerboard,
  half-trapezoid inlays, *P* inlay at 12th fret, decal
  logo.
- **Pickups & Controls:** 2 exposed-coil humbucking
  pickups or 2 P-90 pickups, 4 knobs, selector
  switch on upper bass bout.

ES-175 Aged Reissue (2002–04): Zigzag tailpiece,
aged hardware.

Explorer Voodoo (2002–04): Swamp ash body, Juju
finish (black with red wood filler), ebony fingerboard,
voodoo doll inlay at 5th fret (no other inlays), red
logo, red/black pickup coils.

Explorer Pro (2002–05, 2007–current)
*Angular body, ⅞ of standard Explorer size, flame
maple top*
- **Body & Hardware:** angular-design mahogany
  solidbody, ⅞ of standard Explorer size, flame
  maple top optional, Tune-o-matic bridge, Antique
  binding, chrome-plated hardware.
- **Neck:** mahogany, bound rosewood fingerboard,
  dot inlays, curved peghead with 6-on-a-side tuner
  configuration, pearl logo.
- **Pickups & Controls:** 2 exposed-coil humbucking
  pickups, 3 knobs in line parallel to edge of guitar,
  selector switch on treble horn.

Flying V Custom (2002, 2004): Knobs in straight line,
ebony fingerboard, pearl block inlays, Ebony (2002)
or Classic White (2004) finish. Production: 40 (2002).

Flying V Mirror Pickguard (2002): Mirror pickguard,
Cherry, Ebony or Classic White finish.

Flying V Voodoo (2002): Swamp ash body, Juju
finish (black with red wood filler), ebony fingerboard,
voodoo doll inlay at 5th fret (no other inlays), red
logo, red/black pickup coils.

Gary Rossington Les Paul (2002): Replica of
Rossington's '59 Les Paul Standard, aged nickel-

plated hardware, 2 screws in headstock, Schaller tuners (with holes from original Klusons), aged Sunburst finish, large wear spot on back. Production: 250.

Herb Ellis Signature ES-165 Plus (2002–04): Curly top, removable f-hole inserts, 2 humbucking pickups mounted in top, 4 knobs, selector switch on upper bass bout.

Indian Chief Les Paul (2002): Features from Indian motorcycles.
Production: 100.

John Lennon J-160E Peace (2002): Natural finish. Production: 750.

J-160 Standard (2002) **/ J-160 VS Standard** (2002, 2005–current): See earlier listing for J-160E 1954.

Larry Carlton ES-335 (2002–current): Chrome-plated hardware, small block inlays, slim neck profile, "Carltonburst" finish (yellow-to-red Sunburst).

Les Paul Standard Premium Plus (2002–current): Highly flamed top.

Les Paul Voodoo (2002–04)
Single-cut solidbody, carved top, voodoo doll on fingerboard
- **Body & Hardware:** single-cutaway swamp ash solidbody, carved top, Juju finish (black with red wood filler), black hardware.
- **Neck:** ebony fingerboard, voodoo doll inlay at 5th fret (no other inlays), red logo.
- **Pickups & Controls:** 2 humbucking pickups with red/black coils.

Mahogany Explorer (2002–03): Green, copper, blue and silver satin metallic finishes. Production: 15 in each finish.

Mahogany Flying V (2002–04): Mahogany neck and body, green, copper, blue and silver satin metallic finishes.
Production: 15 in each finish.

Mahogany Futura (2002–04): See earlier listing for Futura Reissue 1996.

Non-reverse Firebird (2002–04)
Solidbody with bass horn longer than treble, humbuckers with polepieces, uniform finish
- **Body & Hardware:** bass horn larger than treble horn, Tune-o-matic bridge, Cardinal Red, Walnut or Pthalo Blue finish.
- **Neck:** set neck, unbound rosewood fingerboard, dot inlay.
- **Pickups & Controls:** 2 humbucking pickups with 2 rows of polepieces, 4 knobs.

Non-reverse Firebird Plus (2002)
Solidbody with bass horn longer than treble, humbuckers with polepieces, swirl finish
- **Body & Electronics:** mahogany solidbody, bass horn longer than treble horn, Blue, red or green swirl finish, some with brushed aluminum pickguard.
- **Neck:** unbound ebony fingerboard, dot inlays, peghead finish matches body.
- **Pickups & Controls:** 2 humbucking pickups, 4 knobs, some with coil tap.
Production: 60 of each color.

SG Special Faded (2002–current): worn Cherry or worn brown finish, 2 exposed-coil humbuckers, unbound rosewood fingerboard, decal logo, Worn Cherry or Worn Brown finish.

SG Voodoo (2002–04)
Double-cut solidbody, pointed horns, voodoo doll on fingerboard
- **Body & Hardware:** single-cutaway swamp ash solidbody, carved top, Juju finish (black with red wood filler), black hardware.
- **Neck:** ebony fingerboard, voodoo doll inlay at 5th fret (no other inlays), red logo.

'02

- **Pickups & Controls:** 2 humbucking pickups with red/black coils.

'52 Les Paul Gold-top Aged (2002): Aged finish and hardware.
Production: 50.

1959 ES-335 DOT Reissue (2002–current): Custom Shop model, dot inlays, plain-top, nickel-plated hardware, single-ring tuner buttons.

1963 ES-335 Block Reissue (2002–current): Custom shop model, small block inlays, nickel-plated hardware, double-ring tuner buttons.

2003

Allen Collins Explorer (2003): Based on 1958 version, Signature model for Lynyrd Skynyrd band member, Korina body and neck, Maestro vibrato, additional strap button on neck heel, aged Natural finish, belt buckle wear on back.
Production: 100.

Chevrolet SSR (2003): Based on CS-336, features from Chevrolet pickup/roadster model. Production: 25.

Copperhead SG (2003): Features from 1967 Chevrolet Copperhead pickup truck including snakeskin carving on top of guitar, *COPPERHEAD* inlay on fingerboard.
Production: 25.

Crazy Horse Les Paul (2003): Features from Parnelli-period Ford Bronco vehicle including tire tread, unbound fingerboard, trapezoid inlays.
Production: 25.

CS-356 (2003–current)
Thinbody double-cut archtop, rounded horns, smaller body than ES-335, block inlays

- **Body & Hardware:** 13½-inch double-cutaway semi-hollowbody, routed mahogany back with solid center area, arched (routed) figured maple top, *f*-holes, rounded double cutaways, body lines similar to ES-335, back beveled on bass side, Tune-o-matic bridge, optional Bigsby vibrato, bound top and back, gold-plated hardware.
- **Neck:** bound rosewood fingerboard, pearl block inlays, decal logo, 5-piece split-diamond peghead inlay, sealed-back tuners, gold-plated hardware.
- **Pickups & Controls:** 2 '57 Classic humbucking pickups, 4 knobs.

Duane Allman (2003): Based on 1959 Les Paul Standard, highly flamed top, Grover Rotomatic tuners, *Duane* spelled out in fretwire on back of guitar.

ES-333 (2003–05)
Thin double-cut archtop, rounded horns, no pickguard

- **Body & Hardware:** thindouble-cutaway semi-hollowbody of laminated maple/poplar/maple, Tune-o-matic bridge, bound top and back, nickel-plated hardware.
- **Neck:** bound rosewood fingerboard, dot inlays, no peghead ornament, decal logo.
- **Pickups & Controls:** 2 exposed-coil humbucking pickups, 4 knobs.

ES-345 Reissue (2003–current): See earlier listing 1959.

ES-446s (2003–04)
Thinbody single-cut archtop, pointed horn, spruce top

- **Body & Hardware:** single pointed cutaway, carved spruce top with integral braces, mahogany back, *f*-holes, Tune-o-matic bridge, trapeze tailpiece.
- **Neck:** unbound rosewood fingerboard, dot inlay.
- **Pickups & Controls:** 2 humbucking pickups, 4 knobs, selector switch on upper bass bout.

Explorer Satin Finish (2003–04): Mon-gloss finish.

Firebird VII non-reverse (2003–04): 3 mini-humbucking or 3 P-90 pickups, gold-plated hardware, unbound rosewood fingerboard, dot inlays, Limed TV finish.

Gary Rossington SG (2003): Early 1960s SG Standard specs, Maestro vibrola, aged and faded Cherry finish.
Production: 250.

Hummer Les Paul (2003 –04): Based on single-cutaway Les Paul Special, 2 humbucking pickups, features from Hummer automobile, yellow finish.
Production: 100.

Joe Perry Boneyard Les Paul (2003–current): Flamed top, weight-relieved body, aged nickel-plated hardware, optional Bigsby vibrato, Boneyard (hot sauce) logo on peghead, signature on truss-rod cover, Custom Authentic Green Tiger finish.

Johnny A. Signature (2003–current)
Double-cut archtop, pointed horns, gamba soundholes
- **Body & Hardware:** thin hollowbody with double pointed cutaways, carved maple top, solid mahogany back and rims, gamba soundholes, Tune-o-matic bridge, stopbar or Bigsby vibrato, bound top and back, gold-plated hardware.
- **Neck:** mahogany, 25½-inch scale, bound ebony fingerboard, custom 3-piece pearl inlay, signature on truss-rod cover, bound peghead, custom pearl peghead inlay, pearl logo.
- **Pickups & Controls:** 2 humbucking pickups, 4 knobs, selector switch near knobs.

Lee Ritenour L-5 Signature (2003–current)
Single-cut archtop, rounded horn, scaled-down L-5
As L-5 Signature with floating pickup, TP-6 fine-tune tailpiece.

Les Paul Acoustic Plain-top (2003–05): See earlier listing 2001.

Les Paul Standard Doublecut w/P-90s (2003–05): P-90 pickups.

Les Paul Diamond (2003–05)
Single-cut solidbody, relief-carved top with diamond pattern
- **Body & Hardware:** single-cutaway solidbody, mahogany back, maple top cap carved with relief diamond pattern, gold-plated hardware, 2-tone finish.
- **Neck:** bound rosewood fingerboard, trapezoid inlays.
- **Pickups & Controls:** 2 humbucking pickups, 4 knobs, selector switch on upper bass bout.

Les Paul Faded Doublecut (2003–current)
Double-cut solidbody, flat top, faded finish
- **Body & Hardware:** double-cutaway solid mahogany body, flat top, rounded horns (like 1959 Les Paul Special), Tune-o-matic bridge, chrome-plated hardware, Worn Cherry, Worn Yellow or satin Ebony finish.
- **Neck:** unbound rosewood fingerboard, dot inlays, Les Paul silkscreen on peghead, decal logo.
- **Pickups & Controls:** 2 soapbar P-90 pickups, 4 knobs, 1 switch.

Les Paul Flame (2003–05)
Single-cut solidbody, relief-carved top with flame pattern
- **Body & Hardware:** single-cutaway solidbody, mahogany back, maple top cap carved with relief flame pattern, gold-plated hardware, 2-tone finish.
- **Neck:** bound rosewood fingerboard, trapezoid inlays.
- **Pickups & Controls:** 2 humbucking pickups, 4 knobs, selector switch on upper bass bout.

Les Paul Smartwood Studio (2003–current)
Single-cut solidbody, carved top, green leaf on truss-rod cover

- **Body & Hardware:** single-cutaway solidbody of certified muira piranga wood, gold-plated hardware, Natural finish.
- **Neck:** unbound muira piranga fingerboard, dot inlays, green leaf on truss-rod cover.
- **Pickups & Controls:** 2 humbucking pickups, 4 knobs, selector switch on upper bass bout.

Les Paul Swamp Ash Studio (2003–current): Swamp ash body, no binding, rosewood fingerboard, dot inlays, Natural finish.

Les Paul Supreme (2003–current)
Single-cut solidbody, carved top, all curly maple, globe on peghead
- **Body & Hardware:** single-cutaway solidbody, carved top, body covered in curly maple veneer, no back coverplates, Tune-o-matic bridge, 7-ply top binding, 3-ply back binding gold-plated hardware.
- **Neck:** bound ebony fingerboard, pearl split block inlays, metal truss-rod cover, peghead inlay of "Supreme" banner around globe.
- **Pickups & Controls:** 2 humbucking pickups, 4 knobs, selector switch on upper bass bout.

Mahogany Explorer Split Headstock (2003–04): Mahogany body and neck, V-shaped headstock.

Playboy Hottie SG (2003–04): Based on SG Standard, 2 humbucking pickups, image of sexy woman on body, *Playboy* bunny head logo on peghead, red finish.

Playboy CS-356 (2003–04): Alpine White finish, silver *Playboy* magazine bunny head logo on body.

Playboy Rabbit Head CS-356 (2003–04): Ebony/white finish.
Production: 50.

The Log (2003)
Replica of Les Paul's Log, 4 x 4-inch centerpiece

- **Body & Hardware:** solid 4 x 4-inch center block, detachable wings from full-depth archtop, homemade vibrato.
- **Neck:** rosewood fingerboard with varied-pattern inlay (originally from a Larson Bros. guitar), 7-piece star-shaped peghead inlay (from 1930s Gibson L-12 acoustic), Epiphone tuners.
- **Pickups & Controls:** 2 pickups with brown oblong covers.
Production: 3.

Tom DeLonge Signature (2003–current)
Thinbody double-cut archtop, rounded horns, 1 pickup, racing stripe
- **Body & Hardware:** ES-335 style semi-hollowbody, Tune-o-matic bridge, bound top and back, brown finish with cream racing stripes.
- **Neck:** bound rosewood fingerboard, dot inlays, Natural finish peghead.
- **Pickups & Controls:** 1 exposed-coil Dirty Fingers humbucking pickup, 1 volume knob.

X-Factor V (2003–current): See earlier listing Flying V 1958.

X-Factor V Faded (2003–current): Rosewood fingerboard, 2 exposed-coil humbuckers, three knobs in triangular configuration, Worn Cherry finish.

10th Anniversary CS-356 (2003–2004): Diamond White Sparkle finish, white pickguard, ebony fingerboard, pearl block inlays, *10th Anniversary* at 12th fret, gold-plated hardware. Production: 20.

10th Anniversary L-4 Thinline (2003): Diamond White Sparkle finish, white pickguard, ebony fingerboard, pearl block inlays, *10th Anniversary* at 12th fret, gold-plated hardware. Production: 30

10th Anniversary SG Custom (2003–04): Diamond White Sparkle finish, white pickguard, ebony fingerboard, pearl block inlays, *10th Anniversary* at 12th fret, gold-plated hardware: Production 40.

10th Anniversary '68 Les Paul Custom (2003): Diamond White Sparkle finish, white pickguard, ebony fingerboard, pearl block inlays, *10th Anniversary* at 12th fret, gold-plated hardware Production: 30.

50th Anniversary Les Paul Corvette (2003): Based on double-cutaway Les Paul Special, scoop carved into top, 2 black soapbar P-90 pickups, 50th Anniversary logo on top, ebony fingerboard with Corvette script inlay, Tune-o-matic bridge, strings anchor through body, chrome-plated hardware, pearl logo, Corvette 50th Anniversary Red finish.

2004

Firebird Studio (2004–current)
Solidbody with treble horn longer than bass horn, smaller than standard Firebird
- **Body & Hardware:** mahogany body shorter than standard Firebird, Tune-o-matic bridge, stopbar tailpiece, chrome or gold-plated hardware.
- **Neck:** set neck, unbound rosewood fingerboard, dot inlays, reverse headstock, logo on truss-rod cover.
- **Pickups & Controls:** 2 standard humbucking pickups, 4 knobs.

Flying V Standard Quilt Top (2004–06): Quilted maple top cap.

Jimmy Page Les Paul, 2nd version (2004–current): Covered humbucker in neck position, exposed-coil in bridge, Pageburst finish. Production: 25 signed, 150 with Tom Murphy aging, unlimited with Custom Authentic finish.

Lee Roy Parnell CS-336 (2004): Custom fat-profile neck, aged nickel hardware.

Les Paul Studio Baritone (2004–05): 28-inch scale, unbound fingerboard, dot inlays, Sunrise Orange, Pewter Metallic or black finish.

L-4CES Mahogany (2004–06): See earlier listing 1958.

Pioneer Cutaway (2004–current)
Thin acoustic solidbody, cutaway dreadnought shape
- **Body & Hardware:** 16-inch dreadnought cutaway (acoustic style) shape, thin body, routed mahogany back, spruce top, "upper belly" bridge with bridge pins, black pickguard.
- **Neck:** bound rosewood fingerboard, dot inlay.
- **Pickups & Controls:** piezo under-saddle pickup, controls on rim.

Ranger (2004–current)
Thin acoustic solidbody, small L-00 shape
- **Body & Hardware:** 14½-inch acoustic body style (like prewar L-00), thin body, routed mahogany back, spruce top, "upper belly" bridge with bridge pins, satin Natural or Saddle Brown finish.
- **Neck:** unbound rosewood fingerboard, dot inlay.
- **Pickups & Controls:** piezo under-saddle pickup, controls on rim.

SG Elegant Quilt Top (2004–06)
Double-cut solidbody, pointed horns, quilted maple top
- **Body & Hardware:** mahogany double-cutaway with pointed horns, quilted maple top, gold-plated hardware.
- **Neck:** bound rosewood fingerboard, abalone trapezoid block inlays.
- **Pickups & Controls:** 2 humbucking pickups, 4 knobs, selector switch.

SG Special Reissue (2004–current): Small pickguard, 2 soapbar P-90 pickups.

SG Standard (Custom shop version 2004–current): See earlier listing Les Paul/SG Standard Reissue 2001.

Slash Les Paul Signature (2004–current): Plain maple top, aged nickel-plated hardware, 2 Seymour

Duncan Alnico Pro II humbucking pickups, Fishman Powerbridge pickup, 3 volume controls, 1 master tone, 3-way switch, 3-way mini-toggle for bridge pickup, Custom Authentic Dark Tobaccoburst finish.

X-plorer Studio (2004)
Angular body, ⅞ of standard Explorer size

- **Body & Hardware:** angular-design poplar solidbody, Tune-o-matic bridge, no pickguard.
- **Neck:** mahogany, unbound rosewood fingerboard, dot inlays, curved peghead with 6-on-a-side tuner configuration, pearl logo.
- **Pickups & Controls:** 2 exposed-coil humbucking pickups, 3 knobs in line parallel to edge of guitar, selector switch on treble horn.

Zakk Wylde Camo Bullseye Les Paul

(2004–current): Camouflage bullseye, maple fingerboard.

2005

Alvin Lee "Big Red" ES-335 (2005–current): Based on Lee's 1959 with replaced fingerboard, small block inlays, 2 exposed-coil humbuckers and 1 Seymour Duncan uncovered single-coil in middle position, 3 volume knobs, 2 tone knobs, 1 switch, peace symbol and other Woodstock era graphics, Custom Authentic faded Cherry finish. Production: limited run of 50 with signed certificate, then unlimited production.

Duane Eddy Signature (2005–current)
Single-cut archtop, moustache inlays

- **Body & Hardware:** 16-inch single-cutaway hollowbody of laminated maple, 3-inch deep, *f*-holes, Tune-o-matic bridge, Bigsby vibrato, bound top and back, nickel-plated hardware, Rockabilly Brown finish.
- **Neck:** maple/walnut neck, bond ebony fingerboard, pearl moustache inlay, pearl logo.
- **Pickups & Controls:** 2 custom single-coil

pickups Baggs transducer pickup under bridge, 4 knobs.

Eric Clapton ES-335 (2005): Tune-o-matic bridge with white plastic saddles, small block inlays, long neck tenon, aged chrome and gold-plated hardware, Cherry finish.
Production: 250.

ES-335 Plain '60s Block (2005): Regular production model, plain-top, block inlays, thin 1960s neck profile.

Judas Priest Flying V (2005–current): 1960s styling, Tune-o-matic bridge with plastic saddles, 2 exposed-coil 57 Classic humbuckers, 3 knobs in triangular configuration, Custom Authentic Candy Apple Red finish, certificate signed by K.K. Downing and Glenn Tipton. Production: 30 (sold as a set with Judas Priest SG).

Judas Priest SG (2005–current): Large chrome pickguard, 1 EMG and 2 Gibson 57 Classic exposed-coil humbuckers, custom stud-mounted bridge tailpiece, bound rosewood fingerboard, dot inlay Custom Authentic Ebony finish, certificate signed by K.K. Downing and Glenn Tipton. Production: 30 (sold as a set with Judas Priest Flying V).

Les Paul Standard Faded (2005–current): Exposed-coil pickups, nickel-plated hardware, fat '50s or slim '60s neck, hand-rubbed Sunburst finishes.

Neal Schon Les Paul (2005–current): Carved mahogany top, multiply binding on top, Floyd Rose vibrato, chrome-plated hardware, sculpted neck heel, pearl diamond inlays, bound ebony fingerboard, DiMarzio Fast Track/Fernandes Sustainer neck pickup, Gibson BurstBucker Pro bridge pickup, 4 knobs with push/pull for mid-cut, 3-way switch, 2 mini toggle switches for Sustainer on/off and octave effect, Green Gold, Alpine White or Ebony finish.

SG Supreme '57 Humbucker (2005–2006): See earlier entry for SG Supreme 1999.

Traveling Songwriter (2005–current)
Solidbody acoustic, circular control plate
- **Body & Hardware:** 16-inch wide thin solidbody, single rounded cutaway, spruce top, mahogany back, moustache bridge shape, bridge pins, bound top, tortoise pickguard with two points.
- **Neck:** mahogany, unbound rosewood fingerboard with treble-side extension, dot inlays, gold-plated tuners.
- **Pickups & Controls:** under-saddle pickup, slider controls on circular plate on upper bass bout.

2006

Billy Jo Armstrong Les Paul Junior (2006–current): 1950s specs, single-cutaway, rosewood fingerboard (Ebony with Classic White finish), 1 stacked double-coil H-90 pickup, wraparound tailpiece, Ebony or Classic White finish.

Jimi Hendrix Psychedelic Flying V (2006): Based on 1967 version hand-painted by Hendrix, Maestro vibrato, chrome-plated hardware, witch hat knobs. Production: 150.

Les Paul GT (2006)
Single-cut solidbody, carved top, monochrome finish with flames
- **Body & Hardware:** single-cutaway solidbody, carved maple top, mahogany back, bound top, Tune-o-matic bridge, extended strap buttons, chrome-plated hardware, monochrome flame finishes.
- **Neck:** bound ebony fingerboard, mirror trapezoid inlays, model name on truss-rod cover, Les Paul signature silkscreen on peghead, locking tuners, pearl logo.
- **Pickups & Controls:** 490R chrome and 498T Smoky Coil humbucking pickups, 4 push/pull knobs, high-pass tone filter, coil taps on both pickups.

Les Paul Goddess (2006–current)
Single-cut solidbody, carved top, 2 pickups, 2 knobs
- **Body & Hardware:** single-cutaway solidbody, carved maple top, mahogany back, wraparound bridge, bound top, chrome-plated hardware.
- **Neck:** bound ebony fingerboard, trapezoid inlays, model name on truss-rod cover, Les Paul signature silkscreen on peghead, decal logo.
- **Pickups & Controls:** 2 humbucking pickups with clear bobbins, 1 volume knob, 1 tone knob, selector switch on upper bass bout.

Les Paul Menace (2006–current)
Single-cut solidbody, carved top, fist on fingerboard
- **Body & Hardware:** single-cutaway solidbody, carved maple top with "tribal" routs, mahogany back, Tune-o-matic bridge, black hardware, flat black finish.
- **Neck:** unbound ebony fingerboard, brass fist inlay at 5th fret (no other inlays), brass frets, custom multi-color logo.
- **Pickups & Controls:** 2 exposed-coil Smoky Coil humbucking pickups with brass stud poles, 4 knobs, selector switch on upper bass bout.

Les Paul Special New Century (2006–current): Full-body mirror pickguard, 2 exposed-coil humbucking pickups, unbound ebony fingerboard, mirror dot inlays, mirror headstock, Ebony finish.

Les Paul Studio Premium Plus (2006–current): Figured maple top, gold-plated hardware, cream truss-rod cover, transparent finishes.

Les Paul Vixen (2006–current)
Thin single-cut solidbody, carved top, small diamond inlays
- **Body & Hardware:** thinsingle-cutaway mahogany solidbody with scarfed back, wraparound bridge, chrome-plated hardware, opaque finish colors.

- **Neck:** unbound rosewood fingerboard, small diamond inlays, Les Paul signature silkscreen on peghead, decal logo.
- **Pickups & Controls:** 2 humbucking pickups, 2 knobs, selector switch on upper bass bout.

Pete Townshend Les Paul Deluxe #9 (2006)
Single-cut solidbody, carved top, mini-humbuckers. Custom Shop production.

- **Body & Hardware:** numeral 9 decal on front below bridge, 3-piece maple top, mahogany/poplar /mahogany sandwich back, Heritage Cherry Sunburst finish, chrome-plated hardware, Nashville wide-travel tune-o-matic bridge.
- **Neck:** bound rosewood fingerboard, trapezoid inlays, 3-piece maple neck with volute.
- **Pickups & Controls:** 2 mini-humbuckers and 1 DiMarzio Dual Sound humbucker. 3 volume, 1 master tone, 3-way selector, 2 mini toggles (one taps DiMarzio, other puts it out of phase). Production: 75.

Pete Townshend Les Paul Deluxe (2006): as previous entry, but with numeral 1 decal on front, Wine Red finish.

Pete Townshend Les Paul Deluxe Gold-top (2006): as previous entry, but numeral 3 decal on front, gold-top finish.

SG Custom (2006–current): See earlier entry 1963.

SG Goddess (2006–current)
Double-cut solidbody, pointed horns, red logo

- **Body & Hardware:** double-cutaway solid mahogany body, pointed horns, chrome-plated hardware.
- **Neck:** bound ebony fingerboard, trapezoid inlays, Goddess on truss-rod cover, no peghead ornament, red logo.
- **Pickups & Controls:** 2 exposed-coil humbucking pickups with transparent bobbins, 1 volume, 1 tone, 3-way switch.

SG GT (2006–current)
Double-cut solidbody, pointed horns, white center section

- **Body & Hardware:** double-cutaway solid mahogany body, pointed horns, Tune-o-matic bridge, massive chrome tailpiece, opaque finishes with white center section, chrome-plated hardware.
- **Neck:** bound ebony fingerboard, mirror trapezoid inlays, GT on truss-rod cover, no peghead ornament.
- **Pickups & Controls:** 2 humbucking pickups, 4 knurled knobs, 1 switch, locking cable jack, push/pull for coil tap, high pass tone filter.

SG Menace (2006–current)
Double-cut solidbody, pointed horns, brass knuckles on fingerboard

- **Body & Hardware:** double-cutaway solid mahogany body, pointed horns, Tune-o-matic bridge, tribal body routings, black hardware, flat black finish.
- **Neck:** unbound ebony fingerboard, brass knuckles inlay at 5th fret, no other inlay, special headstock logo, gold-tinted frets.
- **Pickups & Controls:** 2 "smoky coil" humbucking pickups with brass studs, 4 knobs, 1 switch.

SG Special New Century (2006–current): 2 exposed-coil humbuckers, full-body mirror pickguard, ebony fingerboard, mirror dot inlays, Ebony finish.

Vegas High Roller (2006–current)
Thin double-cut archtop, asymmetrical body, block inlays

- **Body & Hardware:** asymmetrical semi-hollowbody with bass horn longer than treble, flat AAA maple top, *f*-holes, mahogany back, 3-ply top binding, gold-plated hardware, Tune-o-matic bridge.
- **Neck:** bound ebony fingerboard, block inlays, six-on-a-side tuner configuration, Gibson logo on truss-rod cover.

- **Pickups & Controls:** 2 humbucking pickups, 1 volume, 1 tone, selector on upper bass bout.

Vegas Standard (2006–current): Diamond-shaped soundholes, single-ply top binding, chrome-plated hardware, split-diamond fingerboard inlays.

Warren Haynes '58 Les Paul (2006): Based on 1958 Les Paul Standard.

X-plorer New Century (2006–current): Full-body mirror pickguard, rosewood fingerboard, mirror dot inlays, 2 exposed-coil humbuckers.

X-Factor V New Century (2006–current): Mirror dot inlays, full body mirror pickguard.

2007

Elliot Easton Custom SG (2007–current): 2 humbucking pickups, Maestro vibrola with Tiki-man engraved on cover, small pickguard, chrome-plated hardware (Pelham Blue finish) or gold-plated (Classic White finish), left-hand or right-handed.

ES-339 (2007-current)
Thin small-bodied double-cut archtop, rounded horns, two humbuckers
- **Body & Hardware:** thindouble-cutaway semi-hollowbody of laminated maple/poplar/maple designed to lines of ES-335 but with reduced size, Tune-o-matic bridge, bound top and back, nickel-plated hardware.
- **Pickups & Controls:** 2 '57 Classic humbuckers, 4 knobs, Memphis Tone Circuit.
- **Neck:** bound rosewood fingerboard, dot inlays, Kluson-style tuners.

Jimmy Page Double Neck (2007): Mahogany solidbody, pointed horns, 2 exposed-coil humbucking pickups on 6-string neck, VOS (Vintage Original Spec) finish treatment. Production 25 aged to match

Page's original and signed by Page, 250 additional.

Jimmy Page EDS-1275 Double Neck (2007): Mahogany solidbody, pointed horns, 2 exposed-coil humbucking pickups on 6-string neck, VOS (Vintage Original Spec) finish treatment. Production 25 aged to match Page's original and signed, 250 additional.

John Sykes Les Paul Custom (2007): Based on 1978 Les Paul Custom, exposed-coil Dirty Fingers humbucking pickup in bridge position, exposed-coil '57 Classic humbucker in neck position, 4 knobs with bridge-pickup tone control disabled, chrome pickup mounting rings, mirror pickguard, brass nut, chrome-plated hardware, Ebony finish, available aged or non-aged.

Kiefer Sutherland KS-336 (2007–current): *Double-cutaway, smaller than ES-335, double slashed-block inlays*
- **Body & Hardware:** 13½-inch double-cutaway semi-hollowbody, routed mahogany back with solid center area, carved maple top, "Kiefer Gold" aged gold-top finish.
- **Neck:** ebony fingerboard, double-slashed block inlays, bone nut, crown peghead ornament.
- **Pickups & Controls:** 2 '57 Classic humbuckers, 4 knobs.

Les Paul BFG (2007–current)
Single-cut solidbody, carved top, P-90 and zebra-coil pickups
- **Body & Hardware:** single-cutaway solidbody, carved top, no top figuration, no binding, distressed black or gunmetal hardware, transparent finishes.
- **Neck:** unbound rosewood fingerboard, no inlays, no truss-rod cover, distressed black chrome or gunmetal hardware.
- **Pickups & Controls:** P-90 neck pickup, zebra-coil, humbucker bridge pickup, 2 volume knobs, 1 tone control, "kill switch" toggle, selector switch on upper bass bout, no tips on switches.

Les Paul Classic Antique (2007–current): Flamed top, exposed-coil '57 Classic humbucking pickups, rosewood fingerboard, Antiqued binding crown peghead inlay (no Les Paul silkscreen), nickel-plated hardware.

Les Paul Classic Custom (2007–current): Exposed-coil '57 Classic humbucking pickups with gold polepieces, ebony fingerboard, multiply binding, crown peghead inlay (no Les Paul silkscreen), gold-plated hardware, Antique Ebony finish.

DIGITIZED AND AUTOMATED
THE HD.6X-PRO AND ROBOT GUITAR

Since the early 1980s digital technology has made its mark on many corners of the musical instrument industry, making itself felt first in the realms of effects processing and hard-disk recording, then expanding the tonal possibilities of amplifiers in a new breed of 'modeling' amps, and finally arriving in guitars themselves in the 21st century.

Gibson's entry into the digital guitar world was in development for many years before it finally began to glimpse the light of day late in 2006, to be officially released early in 2007 in the form of the HD.6X-Pro Digital Les Paul. Although it wasn't the first digital guitar to hit the scene (the Variax by digital amp maker Line 6 was probably the best received example of the breed up to this point), the HD.6X-Pro offered sky's-the-limit versatility that could be maximized by outboard systems, rather than being limited by the onboard 'menu' of sound selections that many other digital guitars relied upon, and in addition performed as a straight-ahead analog Les Paul Standard when desired.

In addition to two traditional magnetic humbucking pickups, the HD.6X-Pro carries an innovative new Hex pickup, forming the link between analog and digital in the system and comprised of six small individual humbucking pickups. Each of these sends a signal from an individual string to the guitar's onboard, studio-grade, preamps and converters, where these signals are converted from analog to digital, and sent down an Ethernet cable to a proprietary Break out Box (BoB). From here the player can route the output to be processed externally in mono, stereo (splitting the three lower strings and three higher strings), or as six individual signals – one per string. The HD.6X-Pro's onboard preamp system also includes a headphone output for in-ear monitoring, and a facility to return a monitor feed from an external mixer via the BoB and Ethernet cable.

At the end of 2007 Gibson took another leap into the future with the release of the Gibson Robot Guitar, an instrument with fully automated self-tuning capabilities. Like the HD.6X-Pro, the Robot Guitar is a traditional Les Paul Standard that functions entirely as a normal, analog guitar, but is equipped with the PowerTune automatic tuning system. This system contains a built-in pitch-sensing and mechanized adjustment system that literally tunes the guitar for you. It is operated solely from the guitar, with no external connections or interface from a third-party device. A Master-Control Knob (MCK) – which performs like a standard Tone knob in its down position – provides selections between standard tuning, Open E, Dropped D, DADGAD, Open G, Hendrix Tuning (half-step down) or any of a player's own custom tunings. To activate it, the player simply turn to the desired selection, presses the MCK, strums the strings, and the six individual electronic motors in the tuners rotate to bring the guitar to pitch. At the time of writing, Gibson was considering offering the PowerTune system on other guitar models.

2007

'07

THE ES-339: SHRINKING THE SEMINAL SEMI-ACOUSTIC

Gibson has played around with its classic formats plenty over the years – sometimes creating new beauties, sometimes beasts – but 2007's redraw of the ES-335 took a slightly different approach, and a clever one at that, to the usual 'hot-rodding' that the modification of an existing model entailed. For the new ES-339 the Custom Shop retained the iconic shape and proportions of the ES-335, and used similar construction techniques and laminated maple top, back, and sides with a solid maple center block and mahogany neck, but designed a body that was smaller overall, and therefore lighter and easier for many players to get to grips with. The reduced acoustic element in this updated semi-acoustic design also helped to further reduce feedback, one of the original goals of the ES-335 of 1958.

At a glance, the ES-339 looks wholly like an early ES-335 in fact, with its nickel-covered '57 classic humbucking pickups, ABR-1 bridge and dot fingerboard position markers. The only outward clue that this is something new, aside from the size, is the repositioned jack, which has been moved from the front of the guitar to the side. Another minor, but significant, modification to the format is the inclusion of Gibson's Memphis Tone Circuit, which preserves the guitar's high end as the volume pots are turned down.

Les Paul HD.6X-Pro Digital (2007–current)
Single-cut solidbody, carved top, two humbuckers and Hex pickup, digital interface
- **Body & Hardware:** single-cutaway solidbody, carved top, metallic blue finish, silver binding, Tune-o-matic bridge, platinum finished hardware.
- **Neck:** ebony fingerboard, carbon fiber block inlays, platinum truss-rod cover, knurled knob tuners.
- **Pickups & Controls:** 490R neck pickup and 498T bridge pickup plus Gibson Hex Pickup connected to digital interface, 4 knobs.

Les Paul Melody Maker (2007–current)
Single-cut solidbody, narrow headstock, 1 P-90
- **Body & Hardware:** single cutaway solid mahogany body, Tune-o-matic bridge (earliest with wraparound).
- **Neck:** unbound rosewood fingerboard, dot inlays, narrow headstock, decal logo, chrome-plated hardware.
- **Pickups & Controls:** 1 black "dog-ear" P-90 pickup with non-adjustable polepieces, 2 knobs.

Les Paul Standard Limited Edition (2007): White

binding, nickel-plated hardware, ebony fingerboard, crown peghead inlay (no Les Paul silkscreen), Manhattan Midnight, Pacific Reef Blue, Santa Fe Sunrise, Black Cherry w/cream binding.

Robot Guitar (2007-current)
Single-cut solidbody, carved top, PowerTune auto-tuning system
- **Body & Hardware:** single-cutaway solidbody, carved maple top, mahogany back, bound top, Tune-o-matic bridge with internal sensors for PowerTune system.
- **Neck:** bound ebony fingerboard, trapezoid inlays, model name on truss-rod cover, Les Paul silkscreen on peghead, automated tuners.
- **Pickups & Controls:** two humbucking pickups, 4 knobs, neck-pickup's Tone control doubles as Master Control Knob for PowerTune system when pulled out.

SG Select (2007–current)
Double-cut solidbody, pointed horns, trapezoid inlays, flame maple top
- **Body & Hardware:** double-cutaway solid

mahogany body, pointed horns, flame maple top and back, gold-plated hardware.
- **Neck:** 3-piece flame maple neck, bound rosewood fingerboard with Antique binding, trapezoid inlays, metal truss-rod cover, crown peghead inlay, metal tuner buttons, pearl logo.
- **Pickups & Controls:** 2 humbucking pickups, 4 knobs, 1 switch.

SG Special Faded 3 Pickup (2007–current): 3 humbuckers, 2 knobs, 1 rotary selector switch, plain truss-rod cover, Worn Ebony or Worn White finish.

SG-3 (2007–current)
Double-cut solidbody, pointed horns, 3 humbuckers
- **Body & Hardware:** double-cutaway solid mahogany body, pointed horns, small pickguard does not surround pickups, gold-plated hardware.
- **Neck:** bound rosewood fingerboard with Antiqued binding, trapezoid inlays, crown peghead inlay, plastic keystone tuner buttons plastic.
- **Pickups & Controls:** 3 humbucking pickups, 2 knobs, 6-position rotary selector switch with pointer knob.

index

index

index

index

index

The publishers would like to thank the following for their contributions to this project.

Gibson Facts:
Walter Carter; Dave Hunter.

DVD:
Dave Hunter and Carl Verheyen; Brian Fischer, whose fine collection provided the wonderful instruments seen throughout the DVD, and Stephanie Fischer for troubleshooting in New Hampshire; Colin Mottram and Kathy Plaskitt at Lenzflare Creative Production for shooting, lighting, and authoring the DVD. Thanks also to Gibson Custom for the loan of the 1958 Flying V.

Trademarks. The Gibson logos used on the jacket of this package are registered trademarks of The Gibson Guitar Corporation, used with permission.
Also, throughout the book we have mentioned a number of registered trademark names. Rather than put a trademark or registered symbol next to every occurrence of a trademarked name, we state here that we are using the names only in an editorial fashion and that we do not intend to infringe any trademarks.

Updates? The author and publisher welcome any new information for future editions. Write to: Interactive Gibson, Jawbone, 2A Union Court, 20-22 Union Road, London SW4 6JP, England. Or you can email: intergibson@jawbonepress.com.